MW01250997

THE SUMMIT HOUSE MYSTERY

OR

THE EARTHLY PURGATORY

BY

L. DOUGALL

AUTHOR OF

"BEGGARS ALL," "THE MADONNA OF A DAY,"
"THE ZEIT-GEIST," ETC.

FUNK & WAGNALLS COMPANY
NEW YORK
1905

Book I

THE EARTHLY PURGATORY

CHAPTER I

IN the southern part of the Appalachian Mountains the tree-clad ridges fold and coil about
one another. In this wooded wilderness the
trend of each slope, the meandering of each
stream, take unlooked-for turnings, and the
valleys cross and twist. It is such a region as
we often find in dreams, where the unexpected
bars the way or opens out into falling vistas
down which our souls must speed, chasing some
hope or chased by unknown fears.

On a certain day a man called Neil Durgan
passed through the village of Deer Cove, in the
mountains of Northern Georgia. When he had
left the few wooden buildings and the mill
round which they clustered, he took a path by the
foaming mill-stream and ascended the mountain
of Deer.

From the end of the sixteenth century till the freeing of the slaves, the Durgans had been one of the proudest and richest families of Georgia. This man was the present head of the house, sole heir to the loss of all its lands and wealth. He was growing old now. Disappointment, Poverty, and Humility walked with him. Yet Joy, the fugitive, peeped at him through the leafless forest, from the snow-flakes of the dogwood and from the violets in the moss, laughed at him in the mountain torrent, and wooed him with the scent of the warming earth. Humility caught and kissed the fleeting spirit, and led her also in attendance upon the traveller's weary feet.

Deer Cove is more than two thousand feet in altitude; Deer Mountain rises a thousand feet above. Half-way up, Durgan came to the cabin of a negro called Adam. According to the usage of the time, the freedman's surname was Durgan, because he had been born and bred on the Durgan estates. Adam was a huge black negro. He and Durgan had not met since they were boys.

Adam's wife set a good table before the visitor. She was a quadroon, younger, lithe and attractive. Both stood and watched Durgan eat— Adam dumb with pleasure, the negress talking at times with such quick rushes of soft words that attentive listening was necessary.

"Yes, Marse Neil, suh; these ladies as lives up here on Deer, they's here for their health— they is. Very nice ladies they is, too; but they's from the North! They don't know how to treat us niggers right kind as you does, suh! They's allus for sayin' 'please' an' 'thank 'e,' and 'splaining perjinks to Adam an' me. But ef you can't board with these ladies, marsa, ther's no place you can live on Deer—no, there ain't, suh."

Durgan had had his table set before the door, and ate looking at the chaos of valleys, domes, and peaks which, from this height, was open to the view. The characteristic blue haze of the region was over all. The lower valleys in tender leaf had a changeful purple shimmer upon them, as seen in the peacock's plumage. The sun rained down white light from a fleecy sky. The tree-tops of the slope immediately beneath them were red with sap.

After a mood of reflection Durgan said, "You live well. These ladies must pay you well if you can afford dinners like this."

"Yes, Marse Neil, suh; they pays better than any in these parts. Miss Hermie, she's got right smart of sense, too, 'bout money. Miss Birdie, she's more for animals and flowers an' sich ; but they .pays well, they does."

"Look me out two good men to work with me in the mine, Adam."

Adam showed his white teeth in respectful joy. "That's all right, suh."

"Of course, as you are working for these ladies, you will look for my men in your spare time."

"That's all right, suh."

Durgan put down sufficient payment for his food, took up his travelling satchel, and walked on. From the turn of the rough cart-road on which the cabin stood the rocky summit was visible, and close below it the gables of a solitary dwelling.

"A rough perch for northern birds !" said he to himself, and then was plunged again in his own affairs. The branches, arching above, shut out all prospect. He plodded on.

The upper side of the mountain was a bald wall of rock. Where, part way up, the zigzag road abutted on this precipice it met a foot-trail to the summit, and at the same point an outer ledge of flat rock gave access to an excavation near at hand in the precipice. A wooden hut with a rude bench at its door stood on the ledge, the only legacy of a former miner. Durgan perceived that his new sphere was reached. He rested upon the bench and looked about him wistfully.

He was a large, well-built man, with patrician cast of feature, brown skin, and hair that was almost grey. His clothes were beginning to fray at the edges. They were the clothes of a man of fashion whose pockets had long been empty. His manner was haughty, but subdued by that subtle gentleness which failure gives to higher natures. A broken heart, a head carried high—these evoke compassion which can seldom be expressed.

He could look over the foot-hills to where cloud-shadows were slowly sailing upon the blue, billowy reaches of the Georgian plains. In that horizon, dim with sunlight, Durgan had sucked his silver spoon, and possessed all that pertains to the lust of the eye and the pride of life. The cruel war had wrapped him and his in its flames. When it was over he had sought relief in speculation, and time had brought the episode of love. He had fought and lost; he had played and lost; he had married and lost. Out of war and play and love he had brought only himself and such a coat as is as much part of a man as its fur is part of an animal.

After a while he unfolded a letter already well worn. He read it for the last time with the fancy that it was well to end the old life where he hoped to commence the new one.

The letter was written in New York, and dated a month before. It was from his wife.

> "It is very well for you to say that you would not want money from me if I came to live in the south with you, but I do not believe you could earn your own living, and it would ill become my social position to acknowledge a husband who was out at elbows and working like a convict. I think, too, that it is cant for you to preach to me and say that 'it would be well for us to try and do better.' Is it my fault that you have lost all self-respect, refusing to enter good society, to interest yourself in the arts and all that belongs to the spiritual side of life ? Is it my fault that a spiritually minded man has given me the sympathy which you cannot even understand ? I desire that you never again express to me your thoughts about a friendship which is above your comprehension.

"If your rich cousin will let you delve for him for a pittance I shall not interfere. I might tell him he could not put his mine into worse hands! I shall not alter the agreement we made ten years ago, which is that while you remain at a distance, and refrain from annoyance, I shall not seek legal separation."

The husband looked with a faint smile at the crest of the Durgans on the fashionable note-paper, at the handwriting in which a resolute effort at fashion barely concealed a lack of education. In the diction and orthography he discerned the work of a second mind, and it was with a puzzled, as well as a troubled air, that he tore the paper into atoms and let them flutter over the precipice in the soft breeze. But the puzzle was beyond his reading, and the trouble he cast into the past. Whatever good he had deserved at the hands of his wife, it was not in his nature to feel that Providence dealt too hardly with him. As he rose to examine his new scene of work, the phrase of the huge negro returned to his mind, and he muttered to himself, "Yes, suh; that's all right!"

He found a pick and hammer in the shed, and set himself instantly to break the rock where the vein of mica had already been worked. Weary as he soon became, he was glad to suppose that, having failed in dealing with his kind, he must wrestle now only with the solid earth, and in the peace of the wilderness.

The angels, looking down upon him, smiled ; for they know well that the warfare of the world is only escaped by selfishness, not by circumstance.

CHAPTER II

THE sun set glorious over the peaks of the Cherokee ridges, and their crimson outline lay dark, like a haven for the silver boat of the descending moon, when Durgan, satchel in hand, climbed the ascending foot-trail.

The cart-road evidently reached the summit by further turnings; but this footpath, wending through close azalea scrub and under trees, emerged between one gable of the summit house and the higher rocks above it. On the other three sides of the house its open lands were broad enough.

This had been the dwelling of the former miner. Durgan, already heralded by the barking of watch-dogs, could hardly pause to look at a place which would have been his perquisite had it not been bought at a fancy price by woman's caprice.

The low shingled dwelling, weathered and overgrown by vines, was faced by a long, open

Blount, and, of course, we've had dealing with him. That's about the extent of our acquaintance."

She swayed in a light rocking-chair, and for some minutes obviously thought over the request which the letter contained that she should give Durgan a temporary home as a paying guest. He employed the time in looking at books and pictures, which were of no mean quality, but seemed to have been recently collected.

At last she said, "Come to think of it, I don't see why you shouldn't stop with us a while. My sister isn't at home just now, but I guess I'll say 'Yes.' It isn't good for folks to be too much alone. We've a real comfortable room over the harness-room in the carriage-house. You'll have to sleep there, as we've no room in the house, and I guess what we eat will be good enough." A moment's pause and she added, "My sister won't be quite agreeable, perhaps, not being accustomed——"

"Of course, I quite understand, you're not in the habit of doing such a——"

"I did not mean that we felt too grand."

Miss Smith made this answer to his interruption with crisp decision, but as she did not

return to the interrupted subject, he was left uncertain.

While she busied herself for his entertainment,
Durgan, surprised into great contentment, sat
watching the darkness gather beyond the low
arches of the porch. The room was warmed,
and at that hour lit, by logs blazing in an open
chimney. It was furnished with simple comfort
and the material for pleasant occupations. Glass
doors stood open to the mild, still night. The
sweet, cool scent of the living forest wandered
in to meet the fragrance of the burning logs.

There was one uneasy element in Durgan's
sense of rest—he dreaded the advent of the
sister who might not be " quite agreeable."

Out of the gloaming, stooping under the
tendrils of the vine, a young woman came quickly
and stopped upon the threshold. She seemed a
perfect type of womanhood, lovely and vigorous.
One arm was filled with branches of dogwood
bloom, the other hand held in short leash a
mastiff. Her figure, at once lithe and buxom,
her rosy and sun-browned face, soft lips, aquiline
nose, and curly hair gave Durgan sincere
astonishment, although he had formed no expectation. But his attention was quickly focussed
upon an indescribable depth of hope and fear in

her eyes. Before she spoke he had time to notice more consciously the clear brown skin, crimson-tinted on the round of the cheek, the nose delicately formed and curved, and the startled terror and pleading look in her sad brown eyes.

The dog, probably at the suggestion of a nervous movement on the leash, began to growl, and was silenced by a caress as Durgan introduced himself and explained his errand.

"It is very late," she said gravely. "It will surely be difficult for you to find your way down the mountain again."

"Miss Smith has very kindly acceded to my cousin's request." Durgan spoke in the soft, haughty tone of reserve which was habitual to him.

The girl's tone, quick and subdued, had in it the faint echo of a cry. "Oh, I don't think you would like to stay here. Oh, I don't think you——"

Miss Smith came to the door to announce his supper.

"Mr. Durgan is going to stop a while with us, Bertha. It's no use his having a mile's climb from the Cove to his work every day—at least not that I know of. I've been fixing up the room over the carriage-house; I tell him the barns are a sight better built than the house."

It appeared to Durgan that she was reasoning with the younger sister as a too indulgent mother reasons with a spoilt tyrant of the nursery. The effort seemed successful.

Without further comment Bertha said, "We bought this old house along with the ground, but we built the rest. We took great care that they should be good models for the people here, who are rather in need of high standards in barns and—other things."

"In many other things," said Durgan. "I have not been familiar with my own State since the war, and the poverty and sloth I have seen in the last few days sadly shocked me."

Durgan had not of late been accustomed to kindness from women. It was years since he had eaten and talked with such content as he did that evening. If his material comforts were due to the essential motherliness in Miss Smith's nature, it was Bertha's generous beauty and lively mind that gave the added touch of delight. Miss Smith swayed in her rocking-chair, her neat feet tapping the ground, and put in shrewd, kindly remarks; Bertha discussed the prospects of the mine with well-bred ease. Durgan assumed that, as is often the case in the Northern States, the growing wealth of the family had bestowed on the younger a more liberal education than had fallen to the lot of the elder. At the hour for retiring he felt for them both equal respect and equal gratitude.

The stairs to his chamber ran up outside the carriage-house. The room was pleasant—a rainy-day workroom, containing a divan that had been converted into a bed. Books, a shaded lamp, even flowers, were there. As a sick man luxuriates in mere alleviation, as the fugitive basks in temporary safety, so Durgan, who had resigned himself to the buffets of fortune, felt unspeakably content with the present prospect of peace.

He read till late, and, putting out what was by then the only light upon Deer Mountain, he lay long, watching the far blaze of other worlds through the high casement. To his surprise he heard an almost noiseless step come up the stairs; then a breathless listening. He had been given no key, but one was now gently inserted in the lock and turned from without.

Durgan smiled to himself, but the smile grew cynical.

c

CHAPTER III

WHEN Durgan woke in the sunshine the
door had been unlocked and the key
removed.

The sisters, and the good cheer they offered,
were the same at breakfast as on the former
evening; but the incident of the night had
disturbed Durgan's feeling of respect.

Adam and his wife were betimes at their
work as day servants. They had, as commanded,
brought two negro labourers for the mine.
Durgan shouldered his pick and marched before
his men.

They went by the cart-road, under the arching
branches. Suddenly, through the wood, Bertha
appeared, walking alone in the sparkling morning. It seemed a chance meeting till the negroes
had gone on.

Blushing nervously and very grave, she spoke,
begging Durgan to find another lodging. Her
voice, as she gave her reason, faltered. "I am

sure that my sister is not strong enough for the extra care."

Durgan said within himself that the reason was false. He stiffened himself to that dull sense of disappointment to which he was accustomed. " I can only do as you bid me," said he.

"I am afraid you will need to camp out. Believe me, I am very sorry. My sister "— again the voice faltered—" is not very strong. She would try to have visitors for my sake, and so she will not admit that this would be too much—but——"

Again Durgan was sure that her reason was in some way false. This woman was so honest that her very lies were transparent.

"And so—and on this account, I must ask you, Mr. Durgan, to be good enough to—conceal from my sister that I have made this request."

She dropped her eyes in confusion ; her face was flushed, her hands fluttering as she clasped them restlessly ; but she was perfectly resolute.

About her and above the trees were grey. The dogwood alone held out horizontal sprays —white flowers veined in bright mahogany. Above, the sky was blue—a gorgeous blue— and, on a grey bough that hung over, this hue was seen again where the gay bluebird of the south swelled out its glossy crimson throat in song.

As Durgan looked at this beautiful woman and the wild solitude, he felt as deeply puzzled as annoyed. General Durgan Blount had well remarked, as he wrote the letter of introduction, that the presence of a gentleman of Durgan's age and position would certainly appear to be an advantage in the precincts of the lonely dwelling.

"May I ask if you have heard anything to my disadvantage?"

"Oh, nothing! It is for your——" She stopped, her distress growing, but began again very rapidly. "I know it must seem very strange to you; and living alone as we do, it is a great thing for us not to appear odd or strange to anyone. And so—that is the reason I ask you to be so good as——"

She paused, raising her sad eyes for an answering flash of sympathy which his reticence did not give. It was not Durgan's way to give any play to feeling in manner or tone.

Then she said impulsively, "I am trusting you. Don't you see I am trusting you with the secret of my interference? I don't want my sister to know, and I don't want anyone to know, that I have spoken. Hermie would be vexed with me, and other people would think it very odd."

"I thank you for trusting me."

He was lifting his hat and moving when she stayed him.

"I hope you believe that I regret this—that I will do all I can to make your stay on the mountain pleasant for you."

His eyes twinkled. "Pardon me for thinking that you have done all you can to make it unpleasant for me. Your house is not a good one to leave."

"Still, I hope you will remain our friend, and I beg"—she flushed scarlet at her reiteration —"I implore you, when you return for your things, to give my sister no hint that I have interfered, or to speak of it to your cousin."

She went back into the woods, her head bowed. Durgan looked after her with solicitude.

CHAPTER IV

THERE was one other house nearer to the mine than Deer Cove. A small farm belonging to " mountain whites" lay on the other side, but cut off from the road by precipice and torrent. Thither in the early evening Durgan, by steep detour, bent his way, but found his journey useless. The family was in excess of the house-room, and the food obviously unclean.

More weary with his work than labourer bred to toil can ever be, again in the gloaming he climbed to the summit of Deer. He began the ascent with the intention of taking his possessions to the miserable inn at Deer Cove, but on his way reflected that one night more could make little difference to the comfort of the sisters. He would speak to Bertha apart, and ask if he might remain till morning.

The sisters were found together, and Durgan was dumb. Until he was confronted with evidence that Bertha had really given no hint to her sister, he had not realised that, in cancelling the arrangement, much would devolve on his own tact and readiness of excuse. He grew impatient of the mystery, ate the supper that Miss Smith's careful housewifery had prepared, and having no explanation to offer, accepted the early retirement which her compassion for his evident weariness proposed. As on the night before, Bertha offered no opposition.

The work had broken at a touch Durgan's long habit of insomnia. He slept soon and soundly.

Waking in the utter silence of the mountain dawn, his brain proceeded to fresh activities. He reviewed the events of the previous night and morning with more impartial good-nature. From the picture of Miss Smith's motherly age, shrewd wit, equable temper, and solid virtues, he turned to the healthful beauty of the younger sister. He saw again the interview on the road. How transparent her blushes! How deep the hope and terror in her eyes! How false the ring of her tone when she murmured her ostensible excuse! Surely this was a girl who had been sore driven before she lied or asked secrecy of a stranger!

He remembered that the first night someone

had locked him in. A caged feeling roused him to see if he were again a prisoner. He rose, tried the door, and it opened.

Dark ruby fire of the dawn was kindling behind the eastern peaks. Dark as negroes' hair lay the heads and shoulders of all the couchant hills. Their sides were shrouded in moving mists; the valleys were lost; only in one streak of sky above the ruby dawn had the stars begun to fail.

He saw a woman's figure crouching on the porch of the dwelling-house. The wind was moaning.

The woman was sitting on the low flooring of the porch, her feet on the ground, her elbows on her knees, her head held forward, her whole attitude indicative of watching. He thought she slept at her post; or else the wind and darkness covered his slight movement of the door.

Either someone was in great need of compassion, perhaps help, or he was outraged by a surveillance which merited displeasure. He awaited the swift daybreak of the region. Every moment light increased visibly.

When the mists, like white sea-horses, were seen romping down the highways of the valleys;

when the tree-tops were seen tossing and the eastern sky was fleeced with pink, as if the petals of some gigantic rose were shaken out, Durgan went across the grass and confronted Bertha before she could retire.

With a sudden impulse of fear she put her finger to her lips ; then, ashamed, sought to cancel the gesture. She had not changed her gown from the evening before, but was wrapped in furs.

"Last night you locked me in ; to-night you watch my door. What is the matter ? Are you afraid of me ?" He had noticed her abortive signal ; his customary tones met any need for quiet of which he could conceive.

"You !" Her lips formed the word. She seemed confounded by his suddenness. "You !"

He gained no idea from the repeated mono-syllable.

"I will pack up my traps and go at once, rather than rob you of further sleep. Perhaps you will kindly make my excuses to your sister. He was turning, but added, "I evidently owe you an apology for remaining last night. I hope you understand that I had no excuse to give your sister—none, at least, that would not have been too true to suit you or too untrue to suit me."

She made an imperious gesture ; she spoke so low that he wondered at the power of command in her tone. " Go back and take your sleep out —you need it. Come to breakfast without saying that you have seen me. I have no explanation. I have nothing to say—except—" she lifted a weary face—" except that I hoped you were too tired to be wakeful."

His incredulity was overcome by pity. " Can I do you no service ? "

She shook her head. " I have already asked far too much." Her voice sank as she spoke.

" We are neighbours, and I think we must be friends. You are evidently in need of help."

" From heaven—yes. But from you only what I have said."

CHAPTER V

DURGAN furnished the wooden hut that stood on the ledge of the cliff between the road and the mine. Adam's wife baked his bread and made his bed. Durgan fell into the fanciful habit of calling her " Eve."

" Oh, Marse Neil, honey ; Adam an' Eve they was white folks. Thought you'd have known your Bible better 'an us pore niggers, an' we knows that much, sure 'nough—yes, we does, suh."

When Eve spoke, her words came in a multitude, soft and quick.

" Wasn't mighty surprised you didn't stop with those Northern ladies. Very nice ladies they is, but they's the mightiest 'ticlar 'bout their house, an' the workin'est folks I ever did see. 'Taint a sign o' good fam'ly—no, Marse Neil, suh—gettin' up near sun-up in the mornin', and allers a-doin'. 'Taint like quality, an' you couldn't never have stopped. But they's powerful nice ladies, Miss Hermie an' Miss Birdie, an' I don't go to say a word against them, no, suh."

Durgan watched to see if anyone else had a word to say against these ladies. From the loungers of Deer Cove, from the country folk who ascended Deer to sell their produce at the summit house, from the very children who trooped up the road with field flowers and pet animals, he heard the same testimony. In the whole country-side the sisters had the reputation of being gentle and just. Too methodical and thrifty to appear quite liberal in the eyes of the shiftless, too unconscious of the distinction of colour to appear quite genteel, they were yet held in favour, and were to the whole region a source of kindly interest and guileless extortion. No other strangeness was attributed to them than that which "being from the North" implied.

Young Blount, the son of the landowner, soon rode over to see his cousin. The Blounts were one of the few rich southern families who, owning a line of merchant ships, had not lost the source of their wealth in the war. They spent part of their time in this mountain region, of which a large area was their own.

The old General had not changed with the times, but the new epoch had stamped the son with a sense of responsibility for the humanity at his gates which his slave-owning forefathers had never known. He was twenty years younger than Durgan. Having looked upon a devastated land from his schoolroom windows, he had never acquired the patrician manner. He was affable and serious.

When arrived at Durgan's camp, he tied his beautiful horse to a tree, and remained for the night. The two sat on the open rock by a fire of logs. Before darkness fell the visitor had pointed out every village, hamlet, and cabin which lay within the wide prospect which they over-looked.

The inhabitants of this land were, each for his respective station, poor, most of them miserably poor and thriftless. Blount took an interest in each individual. He was a gossip as confirmed as any club-man or idle dowager; but the objects of his interest were not his equals, and their benefit was the end he held in view.

The greenery of the valleys was rising like a tide upon slopes, and merging its verdure in the flush of flowing sap and ruddy buds which coloured the upland forest; but, far and near,

the highest hills still held up their grey wood-
lands to the frosty skies.

After listening to a long chronicle of his
humbler neighbours, Durgan held out his pipe
for a moment, and said casually—

"And the Northern ladies?"

"Ah, yes : despite the Northern flavour, they
are a godsend to the place, if you will! Our
people come from far and near to see their new-
fangled barn, and carriage-house, and kitchen
stoves. It's as elevating to our mountaineers"
—he gave a laugh—"as the summer hotels they
are building in the Tennessee Mountains or at
Nashville are to the people of those parts. A
new idea, an object-lesson. Most useful for
children and fools. Our mountain whites are
obstinate as mules. They think they know
everything because they have never seen anything to rouse their curiosity. You can talk a
new notion into a pig's head sooner than into
them ; but after they have seen an object, fingered
it, and talked it over for a year or two, they imagine
that it had its origin in their own minds. It was a
good enough day for us when these ladies came here;
and then they put some money into circulation."

Durgan, with little further inquiry, soon heard
all that the gossip had to tell.

Miss Bertha, he said, had been delicate. After some years of travel in Europe, a high altitude in a mild climate, and quiet, had been prescribed. A chance of travel had brought them to this place, and the invalid's fancy had fixed itself on this site. Miss Smith, he said, was rather niggardly, but she had recognised that it was worth while to humour her sister's fancy by buying the place.

"She is fanciful then?"

"I did not mean to imply that. You see, there are not many houses in the whole mountain range at this altitude to choose from, and this neighbourhood is quiet and safe. The choice was not unnatural, but I spoke of it being 'humoured' because the General put on a fancy price. He likes to rook a Northerner, and it was not to his interest to separate the house from the mine."

"You would say, then, that they are not fanciful or—eccentric in any way?"

"I should rather say that they have displayed great sense and moderation, never raising a suggestion of their Northern sympathies. They ride about and administer charity in a judicious way. They have even won over the General. Both he and I have a great respect for them.

Their financial affairs are in the hands of an excellent firm of New York lawyers. They have friends who keep up a very regular correspondence. They are both fine women. It is refreshing to come across a little genuine culture in these wilds. I enjoy them every time I call."

In harmony with this last statement, young Blount called at the summit house the next morning, and took his noonday meal with the sisters. When he was riding down the mountain road again he called out, on passing the mine—

"Oh, Neil Durgan—say—why did you leave those quarters? Miss Smith says she gave you leave to stop. Are you anchoriting?"

The unwilling anchorite took comfort in the thought that his discomfort and his silence were offered to, and accepted by, a woman who, for some inscrutable reason, seemed to stand in need of them.

"None so poor but that he has something to give!" he muttered.

CHAPTER VI

THE sisters made all their expeditions on horseback, and, on the upward ride, the horses were commonly breathed on the zigzag of the road which abutted on the mine. Miss Smith, who was disposed to be offended by Durgan's quick change of residence, was dry and formal when he greeted them ; but Bertha bent kind glances upon him, and always made time to chat. Her manner to men had the complete frankness and dignity which is more usually acquired by older women ; and she always appeared to be on perfectly open terms with her sister. Her talk was always replete with interest in the passing events of Deer.

For the first week that Durgan delved he supposed that there were no events on Deer Mountain. Bertha aided him to discover them. She had fraternised closely with her solitudes, not only by directing all things concerning the garden, fields, meadows, and live-stock of the little summit farm, but also by extending her love and sympathy to the whole mountain of Deer and to all the changes in the splendid panorama round about.

"'Nothing happens'!" cried she, playfully echoing Durgan. "Open your eyes, Master Miner, lest by burrowing you become a veritable mole! Can you only recognise the thrill of events when they are printed in a vulgar journal?"

So Durgan's observation was stimulated.

First, there were the events of the weather—what Bertha called the "scene-shifting."

To-day the veil of blue air would be so thin that, in a radius of many miles, the depth of each gorge, the moulding of each peak, was so clear that the covering forest would be revealed like a carpet of fern, each tree·a distinct frond when the eye focussed upon it. The rocky precipices would declare each cave and crevice in sharply outlined shadow, and emerald forms far-off would look so near that house and fence and wandering paths were seen. At such an hour the Cherokee ridges would stand like the great blue-crested waves of ocean, and the "Great Smokies" be like clouds, turquoise-tinted, on the northern horizon.

The next day the azure mists that lay always on the Georgian plain would have crept, embracing the very spurs of Deer, hiding the modelling of even the adjacent mountains as with a luminous gauze. Then only a screen of mountainous outline could be seen, standing flat against emptiness, of uniform tint, coloured like a blue-jay's wing.

Again there was nothing but vapour to be seen, here towering black, here moving fringed with glory and lit within. May showers winged their silver way among the mist-clouds and cleft a passing chasm for the sun.

Or again, following or preceding thunder, there would be an almost terrible clearness of the sun, and big cloud-shadows would flap from range to range like huge black bats with sharply outlined wings.

Secondly, apart from the weather, came startling events in the sphere of what Bertha called "the crops." The term did not relate chiefly to her cultivated land, but to all the successive forms of vegetation upon Deer.

The joy of the opening leaf rose nearer the mountain-top. Already, about Deer Cove, the trees held out a delicate fretwork of tiny leaves between earth and sky, and the under thickets

were tipped at every point with silver-green.
All along the village street a double row of
marsh maples stood, their roots drinking at the
millstream.   The marsh maple differs from its
patient sisters, who are glorified by autumn, and,
like Passion in the house of the Interpreter, in-
sists upon having its good things early.   These
now dressed themselves gorgeously in leaflets of
crimson and pink.   For a day or two this bright
display, seen from afar through the branches that
surrounded Durgan's mine, looked like a garden
of tulips.   Then his landscape narrowed ; his
own trees opened their leaves.   There were days
of warm, quick rain.   Suddenly the grey forest
was glorious with green ; serried ranks of azure
stars stood out in every bank of moss, and the
grey earth was pied with dandelion, heart's-ease,
and violet.

Said Durgan, as the sisters rode by, "Summer
passed me in the night, dripping and bedraggled.
She was going on to you with leaps and bounds."

" ' Dripping,' but not ' bedraggled,' " corrected
Bertha, shaking the mist out of her riding-
gloves.

"Somewhat bedraggled," insisted Durgan.
"Her skirts of wild flowers and meadow grass
are already too long."

But more exciting still were the events of animal life in the purlieus of Deer. The beetles were rolling their mud-balls on the earth; the tadpoles in the mountain ponds were putting forth feet, and the squirrels and birds were arranging their nurseries in different nooks of the greenery above. The polecats prowled boldly to find provender for their wives and little ones. A coon and its cubs were seen. But more interesting than these, because more fully interpreted, were the members of the baby farm over which Bertha reigned. She had calves and kids, litters of pigs and litters of pups, a nest of grey squirrels, nests of birds, and the kit of a wild cat, which a hunter had brought her. This last, a small, whiskered thing, grey as a fox and striped like a tiger, had only just opened its eyes, and must needs be fed from Bertha's hand.

"I am only the grandmother of the others, for they have their own parents," said she; "but I seem to be this one's mother, for it cries continually when I leave it."

For some weeks she carried the kit with her everywhere, even when riding; it curled contentedly in a bag on her lap, and bid fair to be tame.

If Bertha rode out twice a day she paused four

times by the mine to exhibit the growing tame-
ness of her pet, or to recount fresh instances of
the sagacity or prowess displayed by child or
parent in her menagerie.

Durgan went up often to inspect the infant
prodigies, and advise (although he knew nothing)
about their upbringing.

Durgan's own work lay exclusively in the
"mineral kingdom," and he advanced from
ignorance to some degree of skill in auguring
from the bowels of the rock. Each day's work
brought its keen daily interest, each night's sleep
its quota of health and increasing cheerfulness.

CHAPTER VII

WHEN young Blount paid his next visit, Durgan was in a mood better to appreciate his budget of gossip. He even contributed to it.

Adam had beaten his wife, and with good cause. Durgan had himself seen a strange nigger eating Adam's dinner, waited upon by Adam's wife. He found time to explain to his interested cousin that the nigger was both sickly and flashy—a mulatto, consumptive and dandified.

"The worst sort of trash. What could have brought him here? There is no such fellow belonging to the county, I'll swear."

"Adam's wife is not Eve, after all, I think. She can only be Lilith; and I wish the fates would change her for a superior." Durgan spoke musingly.

"At least I hope she'll have more sense than to take a tramping scamp nigger like that to the summit house," said Blount.   "He's sure to be a thief."

"I'd chastise her myself if she did," said Durgan, smoking lazily.

"Ah, I'm glad you feel that way, for those ladies are a real benefit to the neighbourhood, and, to tell the truth, it was on their account I came to you now.   The General sent me."

Durgan smoked on.   They were sitting late at the door of the hut.   Darkness was falling like a mantle over all that lay below their precipice.

Blount began again.   "These ladies from the North can't realise how little our mountain whites know of class distinctions.   If you have only seen one thing, how can you appreciate the difference between that and another ? The mountain men have lived in these hills for generations, knowing only themselves.   You have to be born and bred in the brier bush to understand their ignorance and the self-importance that underlies their passive behaviour."

"So I have heard."

"But Miss Bertha will be getting herself proposed to—indeed she will.   What we are afraid of is that, on that, both sisters will be as angry and unsettled as birds whose nest has been disturbed, and that they will leave the place."

Durgan quite enjoyed his own thrill of curiosity. "Who ?"

"The Godsons, father and son—gardeners, you know—have been laying out a new orchard for the ladies. Young Godson is as fine a fellow as we have at the Cove ; and Miss Bertha has been lending him books, helping to some education, you know."

"Yes ; I have seen them passing—men with blue eyes and rather spiritual faces—father grey, son light brown ?"

"Just so. Fine men if they could have had a chance to look over the hedge of their own potato plot. Miss Bertha has made a protégé of the son. Nothing could be more kind and proper, for she has distinction of manner which could never be misunderstood except by the ignorant. In this case it is doing mischief. The General thought I had better mention it to you."

"Why to me ?"

"Well, we're trying to work up this region. If these ladies were to leave, it would be a distinct loss. If they stay, their friends will visit them ; there is a spell about the beauty of the place ; people with means always return."

"Have they friends ?"

Durgan in lazy manner asked a question he' had asked two weeks before ; the answer was the same. "Very regular correspondence, I understand."

"Is it the money young Godson aspires to ?"

"I am inclined to think it may be love, which is worse ; it would create much more feeling on both sides, for they are women of culture and refinement. That is why we thought you might be willing to warn her."

Durgan mused. He was convinced that the story of the sisters and their solitude was not the simple reading that his cousins supposed ; convinced also that what his cousin called their "culture and refinement" was of a higher cast, because based on higher ethical standards, than the Blounts, father or son, would be likely to understand.

"The affair is not at all in my line." Durgan spoke with haughty indolence. "Why choose me to interfere ?"

"But I assure you young Godson is going ahead. I tell you I positively heard his father chaffing him about her in the post-office ; all the men were about."

"That is intolerable," said Durgan sternly. "What did you do ?"

"It is not as if these men were not given to humorous nonsense between themselves. I could only assume it to be nonsense."

"That would not make it more sufferable."

"I should only have injured my own popularity, and they would have held on their own way. And, after all, if ladies leave their family and choose to live unprotected except by their dogs, it amounts to saying to us and to all that they are able to protect themselves. And," added Blount, "if they knew of this fellow's folly they could protect themselves. The General would ride over any afternoon; but neither he nor I am on terms to broach so delicate a subject."

The answer to Durgan's question, "Why I?" was obviously, "There is no one else." He felt disposed to consider the reason inconclusive till, lying awake that night, he had watched many stars set, one by one, over the purple heights. Thus pondering, he admitted that he was already in a measure Bertha's protector. However inexplicable the circumstance which had given him this office, he could not rid himself of its responsibility. He did not greatly blame young Blount's lack of chivalry in silently hearing the girl's name taken in vain.

Still less did he use the word "duty" of his own intention. He only grew more conscious that, forlorn as his present state was, he had stumbled into a useful relation to this radiant and kindly fellow-creature.

When the next day was declining and Durgan, having dismissed his negroes, was preparing his evening meal, he heard Bertha's step on the narrow trail that, hidden in rocks and shrubs, led from the summit. She paused on a ledge that overlooked his platform, and, holding with one arm to a young fir tree, lowered a basket on the crook of her mountain staff. Framed in a thicket of silver azalea buds, strong and beautiful as a sylvan nymph, she looked down at him, dangling her burden and laughing.

"Pudding !" said she in oracular tone.

"For me ?"

"Pie !" said she.

He lifted a vain hand for what was still above his reach.

Then she lowered the staff with an air of resigned benevolence.

"Pudding and pie. But you don't deserve them, for you were too proud to come to supper, even when I invited you."

"You must remember that to be worthy of my hire I grow stiff by sundown."

She was looking at him now with grave attention. "Have you got a looking-glass?" she asked.

He raised his eyebrows in whimsical alarm.

"If not, you may not have observed how very thin you are growing. Do not kill yourself for hire."

"I shall batten on pudding."

She was retracing her steps when he recalled her. "Will you pardon a word of warning?"

She instantly descended the remainder of the path. It led her round a clump of shrubs, and when he met her at its foot he was startled at the 'change the moment's suspense had worked. She now wore the face of terror he had seen when he caught her guarding his door in the April dawn.

So surprised was he that his speech halted.

She was probably not at all aware of her pallor or dilated eyes. "I am not alarmed," she said. "What is it?" But her breath came quick.

"I must apologise for what may seem an impertinence. I had a little daughter once, and I sometimes think that if she had lived she would have looked like you—let that be my excuse."

"Thank you, indeed ; but what——" She almost tapped her foot in strained impatience.

Then he told her, in guarded terms, that someone had suggested that young Godson did not understand his inferior position.

The look of health and carelessness at once returned to her cheek and eye. "Does that matter ?" she asked. "Living in an isolated place as we do, it is desirable to cultivate friendly relations with one's kind."

It now occurred to him for the first time that for some reason she might be willing to marry below her station. The pathos of her youthful loneliness, even without that additional haunting distress of which he had evidence, lent colour to the new idea.

"Godson is a very fine young fellow ; if he can obtain education he will be most intelligent. He is manly and handsome——"

"But ?" she asked.

"I am perhaps turning busybody in my old age. I thought I saw a difficulty like a snake in your path. If I was mistaken, forgive."

"What sort of venom did you fear ?"

"Presumptuous love."

She stood for half a minute, her face blank with astonishment; then her cheeks flamed; but immediately the look of vital interest died out.

"Truly, I never thought of that." She bit her lip in meditation.

He essayed to speak, but she held up her hand.

"I do not want to know your evidence. I know you would not have spoken unless there was need. Only tell me what I must do."

If Durgan a minute before had felt rueful with regard to his interference, he was now even more unprepared to meet its successful issue.

While he hesitated, she began a quick, practical statement of her case.

"I do not want to estrange any friend, however humble. I stand in need of human friends, as well as of my animals."

"For protection?"

The question came naturally from him; but the moment it was uttered he perceived that she shrank slightly, as if he had broken his compact of silence.

"No; not for protection, but to keep me human. My sister has less need for friends; her religion is everything to her, and she loves

her housekeeping. But with me it is different;
I must get my mind freshened by every human
I come across, and these men have work at
our place for a month to come. I could make
short work of familiarity when it came from
men who know better, but these cannot conceive
that anyone is above them, and so could not see
the justice of reproof. I do not wish to hurt
them, and I dare not make them my enemies.
Tell me what to do."

"If you knew me better, you would not
expect me to guide you. I have made too many
mistakes of my own. My misfortunes are all
my own fault."

"Ah, it is only the saints who say that;
commoners blame the fates or their fellows."

Durgan laughed in sudden surprise. "It is
the first time I have been proposed for such a
society."

"You have been very kind to me," she added
impulsively; "I never expected to find so good
a friend."

He wondered why she should not expect to
find friends, but turned his mind perforce to her
present problem.

"If you could think what it has been in your
dealing with young Godson — what avoidable

touch of graciousness has set his heart on fire,
you might——"

"Oh!" she cried, "I have done nothing;
I have only forgotten—forgotten that for most
people 'love' and 'marriage' are interesting
words. They have no interest for me." As
usual, she regretted an impulsive confession as
soon as she perceived it. "I only mean that
I have no intention of marrying—or rather, that
I intend not to marry."

"Such resolutions are sometimes broken."

"With me that is impossible." Her manner
was growing more remote.

Durgan had not a prying mind, yet he found
his thought full of questions. The more closely
he observed the sisters, the less was he able to
imagine an explanation of what he saw and heard.
Bertha's was a larger intellectual outlook than
her sister's, and it might seem she would weary
of her companion; but, on the contrary, there
was the closest comradeship. Miss Smith
managed the house solely for Bertha's welfare;
but the petted child was not spoiled, and made
every return of unselfish devotion.

E

CHAPTER VIII

CLOSE around the little village of Deer Cove,
three mountain steeps looked down in ever-
lasting peace ; two upland valleys descended to
the village, and held on their fertile slopes
many small farms and hamlets. The houses of
men employed in the saw-mill, which had created
the village, lay within a nearer circle.

Of all this district the post-office at Deer
Cove was the centre. The mill belonged to the
Durgan Blounts, whose summer residence lay at
some distance on the one road which threaded
the descending ravine to the county town of
Hilyard. All substance and knowledge which
came to Deer Cove was hauled up this long
winding road from the unseen town, and halted
at the post-office, which was also the general
store and tavern. Thither the mill-hands, and
an ever-changing group of poor whites, repaired
for all refreshment of body and mind.

The rush of the stream, the whirr of the mill,

the sigh of the wind-swept woods, the never-silent tinkling from the herds that roam the forests—these sounds mingled always with the constant talk that went on in the post-office. Here news of the outer world met with scant attention ; but things concerning the region were discussed, weighed, and measured by the standard of the place. The wealth of a house-keeper was gauged by the goods he received direct from Hilyard and further markets, and his social importance by the number of his letters. A steady correspondence proved stability of connection and character ; a telegram conferred distinction.

In the post-office young Blount, or even the magnificent old General himself, would not scruple to lounge for an hour at mail time, exchanging greetings with all who came thither. Durgan came of stiffer stuff ; he could not unbend. He was also conscious that, as he never received letters, and as his lost lands were here little known, it was only the reflected importance of his cousins that kept him from being reckoned a " no account " person, and suffering the natural rudeness meted out to such unfortunates. He preferred to rely upon Adam to bring him his paper and such news as the village afforded.   Adam went to the post every evening for Miss Smith.

There came a week of rain.   The road to Hilyard was washed away by the first storm. The mail accumulated there, and when at last it could be brought to Deer, it was still raining. Durgan's cutting was flooded.   Unable to work, he had paid a visit to his cousins, and returned one evening, through a thick cloud which clothed Deer like a cerement, to find Adam in the hut by the mine, seated before a hot fire.

In the light of the dancing flame, the big black man, all his clothes and hair dripping and glistening, was indeed a strange picture.   He was wholly intent upon a row of papers and letters, which from time to time he moved carefully and turned before the blaze.

"It's all right, suh.   I only clean done forgot to put the ladies' lettahs in de rubber bag they give me.   It's a debble of a rain to-night, suh ; it soak through all I hab, and there's a powerful lot of lettahs to-night, suh ; a whole week o' lettahs, Marse Neil, so there is."

Durgan looked down at a goodly assortment of mail matter—newspapers, missionary records, magazines, business letters from well-known stores.   In the warmest place was a row of private letters. Adam's big hands hovered over these with awesome care.

"They's the lettahs the ladies is most perjink about, allus." Adam spoke proud of his own powers of distinction. " I'se not worked for 'em so long, suh, widout bein' able to know their 'ticlarities."

"I'm proud of you, Adam." Durgan went out into the mist again and sat on a ledge of rock.

It was still daylight, but the thick mantle of cloud was grey in its depths, toning the light to dusk. Within the circle which the mist left visible, the jewelled verdure showed all its detail as through a concave lens.

It was the hour at which Adam's wife usually came to set Durgan's hut in order. Through the ghostly folds of cloud she now appeared like a beautiful animal, cowering yet nimble, swift and silent, frightened at the loss of all things beyond the short limit of sight, the very pressing nearness of the unknown around the known. Framed in the magnified detail of branch and bole and dewy leaves, Durgan saw her arrive and pause with involuntary stealth in the fire-glow from the door of the hut.

Eve did not see Durgan. As a dog, and

especially a female dog, can worship a master, so Eve worshipped Durgan. When she fawned upon him all her attitudes were winsome, her bright eyes soft, and a gentle play of humour was in her features. Despite his studied indifference and contempt, he had never before seen an evil look upon her face, but now with malicious shrewdness she was observing her unconscious husband.

Suddenly Adam, without turning, uttered a short yell of terror.

Durgan sprang and entered with the woman.

Adam rose from his stooping position—his jaw dropped, his teeth chattering. "As I'm alive, suh, the lettahs they come open of themselves, sittin' right here before the fire ; an' they was so soppin' I jest took the inside out to get it dry. As I'm alive, Marse Neil, suh ; the debble's in this thing. 'Tain't nowise any person but the debble as would send ladies—very nice ladies, too—lettahs like this, with no writin' on 'em ; that's the debble all right, suh, sure enough."

Durgan's gaze had fixed itself involuntarily on the sheets the man had dropped. The envelopes which had purported to hold letters of private friendship had, in truth, held blank paper.

Assured that such was the fact, however strange, Durgan sought some words which might quiet the terrified Adam and efface the circumstance from Eve's frivolous mind. He could trust Adam, when quiet enough, to obey a command of secrecy; the negress must be beguiled.

But she was too quick for him. She was now watching his eyes, reading there part of his interpretation, and with half-animal instinct, perceiving that he desired to hush the matter, thought to make common cause with him.

"You's a sure enough convic' now, Adam chil'; an' I'd like to know who's to be s'portin' o' me when you's workin' out your time in chains. Is you so ignorant, chil', as not to know that it's a heap an' a lot wus to read these letters than the sort as has writin' all ovah?"

The negro's terrified attitude showed some relief. "I didn't know as there was a sort o' lettah that had no writin' on, honey. Is you sure o' that, honey? I thought these lettahs must be a sure enough work o' the debble."

"Sure as I'm a born nigger, there is lettahs o' that sort; an' it's hangin', or somethin' wus, to open 'em. Oh, Adam, it's a powerful hangin' crime; an' if you's cotched in this business, what'll come to me?"

The woman paused to wipe an eye, then—

"I tell you, Adam, your on'y chance o' takin' care o' me any more is nebber so much as to speak o' these lettahs down to Deer or any other place. Because no gen'leman or lady or decen' nigger would ever so much as say that there was this sort o' lettah—'tain't perlite, 'cause it's on'y the great folks, an' the rich, an' the eddicated, as gets 'em. Isn't that gospel truth, Marse Neil, suh?"

Durgan was listening, intent on laying a trap for the wife. He gave no sign.

But Adam, honest soul, too unsuspicious to wait for Durgan's corroboration, spoke with steadily returning confidence. "Sure as I'm stan'in' here, Marse Neil, suh, these lettahs opened themselves—like that yaller flower that comes open of itself in the evenin', suh; an' takin' of them out, I only had the contention, suh, o' dryin' the insides of 'em; for I can't read the sort o' lettah that's written all ovah—only the big print in the Testament; an' the min'ster that learned me, he'll tell you the same."

Eve's voice rose in the soft climax of triumph. "An' that's jest the reason, Adam chil', that readin' o' these lettahs is hangin', an' workin' in chains, an' States prison, an' whippin'—all that jest 'cause niggers like you an' me can't read the other kind." Eve was getting beyond her depth.

"You've learned me somethin' this very hour, honey," said Adam kindly, "for I didn't know before sure enough there was this sort o' lettah; but you degogerate now, honey, for if it's hangin', it can't be work in chains, an' if they can't prove I can read other sort o' lettah, it's mighty powerful sure they can't prove I ken read these. The debble himself ken't prove that."

Durgan had sealing-wax with which he fastened his samples of mica for the post. He put the blank pages back in the envelopes and fastened them with his own seal. Telling Adam to explain only that the flaps had come open in wet, he dismissed him. He sat watching the negress sternly, and she grew less confident.

"Us pore slave niggers don't know nothin', Marse Neil, suh."

"How old are you?" He spoke as beginning a judicial inquiry.

"Us pore slave niggers don't know how old we is. I's gettin' an old woman—I's powerful old. I wus crawlin' out an' aroun' 'fore the 'mancipation. Ole Marse Durgan, he jest naturally licked me hisself one day when I crawled 'fore his hoss in the quarters. That's what my mammy told me. We's all Durgans—Adam's folks an' mine."

"You are no Durgan nigger. I know you. We bought you and your mother out of bad hands." Durgan spoke roughly, but in himself he said, "Alas, who was responsible for this creature, sly and soulless? Not herself or those of her race!"

"Have you seen letters with no writing on them before?"

"Why should a pore nigger know anythin' 'bout such lettahs? If you'll tell me how God A'mighty made the first nigger, I'll tell you as well why these ladies gets lettahs stuffed like that, an' no sooner—an' that's gospel truth, Marse Neil, suh. I's got nothin' to do with white folks' lettahs."

He was sure now that she knew no more than what she had just seen, and had drawn no inference.

She gave way to tears, realising that he did not approve of the address with which she had managed Adam.

"Marse Neil, Adam's a powerful low down nigger, Adam is. He's a no account darkie, is

Adam. You know yourself, suh, how he laid on to me t'other night."

"If he had let you go off with a thieving yellow coon like that other nigger, you might say Adam was unkind—kindest thing he could do to beat you !"

She was so pretty she could not believe any man would really side with her husband against her. "Oh yes, Marse Neil, suh ; I don't go for to say as a darkie shouldn't beat his wife— any decen' Durgan nigger would, suh ; but the thing that's low down, an' dreffle mean, an' no account 'bout Adam is that he don't know when to stop. Lickin'—that's all right, suh ; but when a nigger goes on so long, an' me yellin' on him all the time—oh, Adam, he's a low down feller an' dreffle mean."

"You did more yelling than he did beating. He was crying all the time. I don't believe he hurt you—but go on."

Her tears were unfeigned : she cared only to regain Durgan's good-will.

"Go on with what, suh ?"

"With what you were telling me."

There had certainly been no sequence discernible.

"Well, marsa, a poor girl like me don't go for

to tell lies for nothin'. Nex' time Adam holds a stick over me, I's got the States prison to hold over him. An' you's mistaken, marsa, honey, in sayin' as he didn't maul me black an' blue, for he did, suh—not that it wasn't right an' just this time, as you say so, marsa ; but for nex' time I mus' have a way for to 'scuse myself to him. So you won't go for to tell him it isn't hangin', will you, marsa, honey, suh ?"

The softness and assumed penitence of the low wail with which she ended made Durgan laugh aloud. " Look here. Look me straight in the face ! "

She could do that very well, raising her soft, doe-like eyes to his, then fringing them with her lashes as an accomplished beauty might. Durgan was so angry with her on Adam's account, that he forgot that his first object was to secure her silence.

" You've got a good husband and a good home. If you ar'n't good to Adam after this, I'll despise you. Do you understand ? "

" Don't speak to me so sharp, marsa." There was already a little edge of malice in the velvet of her voice.

" Now, about these letters—if I catch you ever speaking of them again, I'll tell Adam you've lied to him, and why. I'll tell him all about you, and he'll never trust you again.   Do you understand ?"

· "An' if I don't tell nothin' you ain't disposed on, Marse Neil, honey ?"

"Then I'll be kind to you, and let Adam think you're better than you are."

But the negress, turning to her work in the hut, no longer moved about him with liquid eyes and joyful steps, as a happy spaniel does. Beneath her calmer demeanour he saw the shade of sullenness, and still heard the edge of malice in her voice.

"I have been a fool," thought he. "She would have managed better in my place." Then he dismissed her from his thoughts.

CHAPTER IX

THE letters Durgan resealed had each borne a different handwriting; they had not all come from New York. The sheets could hardly have been covered with invisible ink, having been subjected to both water and fire with no result. These, apparently, were the letters which came to the sisters with marked regularity.

"These ladies are hiding," said Durgan to himself. "This is a device of their New York lawyers to save them from remark." He was unable to associate trickery with the sisters.

In considering Bertha's strong repudiation of future marriage, he began to suppose that she might be already unhappily married and hiding from some villain who held her in legal control. But, in that case, why was she more at ease when riding than at home, and why did she betray fear of some danger close at hand?

With nightfall the rain-cloud sank down, and the moon, floating above in an empty sky, showed clear on the mountain-tops. The rock wall above and below Durgan's camp glistened with silver facets, and the wet forest all about shimmered with reflected light.

But, beautiful as was the shining island of Deer in its close converse with the queen of night, it was not so strange a sight as the upper moon-lit levels of the vast cloud which was floating a hundred feet below.

Durgan went up the trail, passed the vine-hung house, and climbed the highest eminence.

The cloud was composed of perpendicular layers of mist, the upper crests of which rolled in ridge over ridge before the wind—a strong surge of deepest foam. So white was each wave that only in its deep recess was there a touch of shadow. The whiteness was dazzling; the silence absolute.

The adjacent mountain-tops were like black islands in mid-ocean.

The silence seemed a terrible thing to the cheated sense of sight. The cloud breakers curled upon the sides of Deer, broke in fragments like wind-blown froth, curled back, and broke again, as if lashing the rocks and forest trees. Up the deep channel of the valley the waves rolled on with a steady rhythm and fall

of surf that should have filled the mountain
spaces with its thunder. Across the shining
flood, against the black shoulders of opposite
shores, the same surf tossed and fell. Yet there
was no echo far or near, or murmur; only the
hush of a phantom world.

Durgan stood long on a portion of the
mountain-top which was covered with short,
scrubby oak in young leaf, fascinated by the
mighty movement and intense silence.

A rustle came near him amongst the covert.
He looked down and stroked the head of one
of Bertha's great dogs. He saw the mistress
coming : she was cloaked and hooded. It was
the hood, perhaps, that hindered her observing
him till she was very near.

She uttered a cry of undisguised terror, throwing out her arm, as if to ward off an expected blow.

This movement of defence, so instinctive, told
Durgan more than any tale of woe the lips could
frame. He was confounded by such evidence of
some scene or scenes of past cruelty.

"Now, in the name of Heaven," he cried,
"what do you fear ? You know that the dogs
would allow no mortal to injure you or yours.
Is it some murderous spectre of whom you stand
in dread ?"

She regained a quiet pose, but seemed dazed by the unexpected fright.

"A murderous spectre! What do you mean? Why do you use that phrase, Mr. Durgan?"

"The words are pure nonsense. I used them to show you how baseless your fear appears. But I speak now in earnest to say that you ought not to come out at night alone if you are thus alarmed."

"But I am perfectly safe with the dogs."

"Just so. Then why were you afraid?"

"I—I—in that shawl mistook you for——" She came to a final pause.

He remembered now that, to shield himself from the drenched verdure, he had wrapped a camp blanket around him.

"Yes, I certainly cut a queer figure—like an old wife; but, pardon my insistence, it is not good for any woman to be so terror-stricken as you were just now. That you are safe from danger with the dogs I truly think; but fear itself is injurious. If you are not safe from unruly fears, why roam where you invite them? It is always possible to meet a stranger."

"Oh, I am not afraid of travellers."

"Any shadow may assume a fantastic form."

"But I am really not afraid of odd appearances."

r

"Then why were you afraid of my blanket?"

But her caution returned. With inconsequence and a touch of reproach she said, "You would rather have the mountain all to yourself, I believe."

"I should be twice desolate. But that has nothing to do with my request that you should keep where you not only are, but feel, safe."

"But if my fears are the result of my own imagination, why should any place be better?"

"You are fencing with me now. If you could tell me what it is you fear——"

She walked by his side as if thinking what she might answer him. "You used a phrase when you just spoke—what put it into your mind?—which perhaps expressed what I fear as literally as words can."

"What do you mean by endorsing such foolish words?"

"Your regard—your friendship, for us, is a very great comfort to us both—the best boon that Providence, if there be a Providence, could have sent us. Yet you have forced me to say what forfeits your regard."

"That would be impossible. Our regard for one another is based solidly upon that touch of good principle which makes the whole world neighbours."

"Ah! I am glad you say that. It is so comfortable to know your benevolence does not depend on our worth. Long ago, and I would have resented such an intimation from anyone; now it gives me the same sort of comfort that a good fire does or, say, a good pudding."

She was regaining her spirts; but there was still a tense ring in her voice which meant intense sincerity.

"Your regard for me has the same basis," said he; and added soon, "I am greatly in earnest in what I say; you ought not to put yourself in the path of fears you cannot master."

"I thank you for the advice. What exactly was it that happened to our letters to-night?"

He ascertained that Adam had given his meagre message discreetly. He could now have comforted her easily with half the truth, but he told all briefly—in whose hands was the keeping of the curious fact of the blank letters, and why he judged it comparatively safe.

Bertha pushed the hood from her head, as if she felt suffocated. She sat down upon a fragment of rock on the verge of the hill, and they both gazed at the silent rolling of the cloud beneath.

" Tricks are folly, and deserve detection," she said at length. " Silence is the only noble form of concealment. Yet our friend, who is a lawyer, told us that if we came here obviously as friend-less as we are, rumour would have been cruel. It would have worried our reputation as a dog worries a rat. Every face we met would have been full of suspicion, and—surely it is right to shun morbid conditions?"

Durgan stood uneasy. " People often drop almost all correspondence through indolence," he suggested.

" My sister permitted the trick, I think, simply for my sake. She was distressed by your seals and hearing that the letters had come open. I shall be able to tell her it did not happen at the post-office."

" I should have thought your sister would have trusted her fate in God's hands with perfect resignation."

" Yes, I think she does. She has great faith in God."

After another pause, he said, " You were so good as to ask me the other day for advice ; will you take an old man's advice now and go home to bed ? All things appear more reasonable by daylight, and the more you tire yourself, the more you are likely to see the circumstances of life in distorted shape."

She answered with an anger that leaped beyond her more tardy self-control. "You know no more than my dogs do what I can and cannot do, what it is drives me here to-night, or what it is that I fear."

"I beg your pardon."

Penitent in a moment, she said, "You are truly kind, Mr. Durgan. I am so glad that we have a neighbour, and that he should be what you are."

"I wish, since you are in misery, that he could have been one in whom you could confide, who could perhaps help."

She stood wrapping her cloak closer about her. "Let me be petulant when I want to be petulant, mysterious when I must, tragic when I must, gay when I can. Let my moods pass you as the winds pass. If you can do this and preserve a secret, you will do more than any other human being could or would." She waited a moment, and added, "I have trusted you from the first to do this; I do not know why."

CHAPTER X

THE mountains now burst into midsummer. Bloom, colour, and fragrance reigned ; also heat and drought. The cups of the tulip tree, the tassels of the chestnut, lit the leafy canopy. The covert of azaleas blazed on the open slopes in all shades of red and yellow. In every crevice by the trickling streams rhododendrons lined the glades with garlands of purple and white.

The hidden house of the sisters was embowered in climbing roses and the passion flower. It was surrounded by gorgeous parterres, and the tendrils of the porch vines hung still, or only fluttered at sundown. There was no vapour at dawn or eve in gorge or on mountain-top. A dry blue haze like wood smoke dulled light and shade in the myriad hills. They looked like a vast perspectiveless painting by some prentice Titan, who had ground his one colour from the pale petals of the wild hydrangea. Some clouds

70

there were—ragged towers, tinted in the light browns and pinks of sea-shells. They tottered round the far horizon in fantastic trains, but came no nearer. The very azure of the sky was faded by the heat of the sun.

All moss and low wild flowers had long withered; the earth under the forest was hot and dry. The whole region basked, and from all the valleys a louder and more ceaseless tinkling rose from the herds of pigs and oxen who roamed for meagre provender.

One afternoon Durgan and his labourers heard a cry. It was the voice of Adam. They heard him crash through the brushwood above them.

"Fire!" yelled Adam, and crashed back toward the summit house.

Durgan outran his men, and was relieved to find the evil not beyond hope of redress. Smoke was issuing from one corner of the roof of the dwelling-house; no flame as yet, but the roof was of shingle, like tinder in the sun.

The ladies, with admirable skill and courage, had already organised their forces—Adam pumping, Bertha and Eve stationed on the path from the well, Miss Smith, the most agile, taking the

bucket at the door and running up the stair.
Thither Durgan followed, leaving his men to
Bertha's command. The fire was smouldering
between the ceiling of the kitchen and a pile
of papers and books which lay on the floor far
under the sloping roof of the low attic. Miss
Smith had been wise enough to move nothing.
The solid parcels of periodicals kept out the air,
and she was dashing the water on the roof and
floor.

With the added help smoke soon ceased. It
remained to investigate the cause of the fire,
which was not obvious, to make sure that the
rest of the house was safe, and undo as far
as possible the injury of the water, which, spread-
ing itself on the attic floor, had poured into the
bedrooms below.

While the negroes were carrying out the
parcels of printed matter, wet and charred,
Durgan moved about in all the recesses of the
house, examining the walls, lifting wet furniture
on to the sunny verandah roof, and otherwise
helping to modify the unaccustomed disorder.

While thus engaged, he realised how strongly
had grown upon him a fancy that these lonely
women might be harbouring some insane person,
whose escape and violence they might justly

dread. He must now smile at himself for thinking that any source of terror lurked here in visible shape. As he followed Miss Smith from one simple room to another, creeping under the very eaves of the roof and feeling the temperature of every wall and shelf, he certainly assured himself that neither the skeleton nor its closet was of material sort.

He was struck with the orderly and cheerful arrangement of the house, with the self-control, speed, and good sense the sisters had displayed ; but most of all was he surprised that the excitement and effort had unnerved them so little. When the hour for relaxation came, they appeared neither talkative nor moody ; they neither shed tears nor were unusually cheerful. In his married life he had had some experience of women's nerves. This calm, practical way of taking a narrow escape from great loss roused his admiration.

Many bundles of papers were too much damaged to be worth keeping. Durgan had a use for these in a stove his labourers used, and, after Miss Smith had looked them over, they were carted down to the mine. Durgan sorted them, storing some old magazines and more solid papers for future use.

He soon found the covers of an old book, tied together over a collection of parchment envelopes. These in turn contained newspaper clippings still legible. Each envelope had its contents marked outside; they were the reports of a number of criminal trials, extending over a number of years, cut from American, English, and other European papers. Durgan was at once convinced that neither of the sisters could have been interested in the collection, and, assuming it to be the work of some dead relative, he reflected for the first time how rarely they spoke of family ties. It was true that Bertha would sometimes say, "My dear father would have enjoyed this view—would have liked this flower," or "Dear papa would have said this or that." He remembered how her voice would soften over these sacred memories, and remembered, too, how they always came to her among the beauties of nature, never in domestic surroundings. Such a father would scarcely have been so much interested in annals of crime.

Sitting by the lamp in his hut, Durgan went over the envelopes. The first was dated ten years before; it contained the notorious Claxton trial, reported by the *New York Tribune*. The next was the case of the Wadham pearls, from the London *Times*. Durgan was not familiar with the case, and became interested in the story of the girl, very young and beautiful, who, being above temptation of poverty and above reproach, had been sentenced, on convincing evidence, for theft and perjury. The common interest in these cases obviously was that in both the accused was a gentlewoman, and the evidence overwhelming, although chiefly circumstantial. The cases that came after did not follow this thread of connection. They were stories of such crimes as may almost be considered accidental, in which respectable people fall a prey to unexpected temptation or sudden mania. The last selection was from the *Galignani Messenger*. It was the case of a parish priest, apparently a *dilettante* and æsthetic personage of highly religious temperament, who was condemned for having killed his sister with sudden brutality, and who gave the apparently insane excuse that, seeing her in the dusk, he had thought her a spirit, and been so terrified that he knew not what he did. The date of this last story was only about three years after the first.

Next day, when Bertha passed by on her horse, Durgan told her what he had found.

"Oh, I am sure we don't want them," said she. "Burn them with the rest."

She was wearing a deep sun-bonnet; he could hardly see her face in its shade.

Durgan had very naturally tried to fit the circumstances of any of these stories of crime to a domestic tragedy which might have resulted in the hiding of these sisters and in Bertha's fears; but none of them seemed to meet the case, nor did any story he could devise.

Since the opening of the letters, and Bertha's words in the moonlight, he had wondered more than once whether she believed in some ghostly enemy. Durgan had been rudely jostled against such fantasies in his domestic experience. His wife was nominally a spiritualist, and although he was inclined, from knowledge of her character, to suppose her faith more a matter of convenience than of conviction, he had reason to think that the man who had long dominated her life under the guise of a spiritual instructor was, or had been, entirely convinced of his own power to communicate with the spirit world. This man had believed himself to see apparitions and hear voices. Durgan did not believe such experiences to be spiritual, but gave more weight to the question of such a belief in Bertha than if he had not already rubbed against the dupe of such a monomania.

The subject was not a pleasant one, yet, in connection with this painful theme, Durgan resolved to speak to Bertha in the hope of inducing confidence and perhaps driving away her fears.

CHAPTER XI

FOR a few days after the fire at the summit
house some of the mountain folk from far
and near took occasion to ride up to the scene of
the excitement, "to visit with" the ladies, and
hear that the bruit of the matter had greatly
magnified it. They were an idle, peaceful
people; a little thing diverted them.

The road by the mine was thus unusually
gay; yet Durgan kept a more or less jealous
watch, and at last caught sight of the yellow
negro who a month before had visited Eve. He
was dressed like a valet, in an odd mixture of
clothes from the wardrobes of a gentleman and
a groom. His features were small and regular;
his long side whiskers had an air of fashion
which did not conceal the symptoms of some
chronic disease.

"Ho!" cried Durgan; "where are you going?"

The darkie stopped with a submissive air,
almost cringing as one accustomed to danger.

"What is your name?"

"'Dolphus, sir—'Dolphus Courthope."

"Courthope?"

"Yes, sir—from New Orleans. Mr. Courthope was very rich and had a great many slaves." He spoke correctly, with a Northern accent.

"*You* never saw slavery," said Durgan in scorn. "You have no right to that name."

"No, sir; my father and mother gave me that name. They belonged to Mr. Courthope."

"You were here before."

"Yes, sir; I came last month, but I went back to Hilyard. I came looking for"—there was just a perceptible pause—"the Miss Smiths; but I thought I'd come to the wrong place."

Durgan felt at a loss. On Adam's account he could have ordered the man off, but he had no right to inquire into his errand to the Smiths.

"I'm a respectable boy, sir. I'm not going to do any harm. I've got business." The darkie made this answer to Durgan's look of suspicion, and spoke with apparent knowledge of the world and confidence in the importance of his errand.

"See that you don't get into mischief!" With this curt dismissal Durgan stepped back into his own place.

In some minutes, when he heard the watchdog

barking above, he went up the short foot-trail, expecting to reach the house with the negro, but nearing it, saw no one without.

From the open windows he heard Bertha's voice raised in excitement. "I will not leave you alone with him, Hermie, you need not ask it. He can have nothing to say that I should not hear."

As Durgan drew nearer he. heard Bertha again, this time with a sob of distress in her voice. "I don't care what he says or does; I will brave anything rather."

"Birdie, darling, you are very, very foolish!" Miss Smith's voice was raised above her natural tone, but was much calmer.

Durgan's step was on the wooden verandah.

Doors and windows were all open to the summer heat. The sisters were standing in the low sitting-room. The negro, hat in hand, stood in a properly respectful attitude near the door. As before, his manner suggested that he was a servant and had no aspiration beyond his sphere.

"I saw that fellow come up the road," said Durgan. "I do not know, of course, what his errand is here; but I thought I ought to tell you that Adam told me that he had got no regular job, and that he had found him idling around a month ago with no apparent reason."

"Yes, sir; I was trying to discover from Adam's wife who it was that lived up here; but she told me so many fixings out of her head about these ladies that I come to the conclusion they wasn't the ladies I was looking for. Miss Smith knows me, sir; and I've been very ill lately —the doctor tells me I'm not long to live."

"Oh, you folks always think you're dying if you've got a cold. You're begging, I see."

"Yes, sir; I was asking this lady to help me. I'm dying of consumption, sir."

The man's manner was quiet enough. Durgan saw that both the sisters were intensely excited. The elder had her emotion perfectly under control; the younger looked almost fierce in the strain of some distress. What surprised him was that his protection was equally unwelcome to both. He could see, spite of their thanks, that, in trouble as they were, their first desire now was that he should be gone.

"I do not trust this man," Durgan said. "I would rather stay within call till you dismiss him."

"I'm all right, sir," said the darkie, again respectfully.

G

"He won't do us any harm," cried Bertha eagerly.

"I know who he is," said Miss Smith; "I know him to be unfortunate, Mr. Durgan."

Yet Durgan saw dismay written on Bertha's face as surely as if they had been attacked by open violence.

"Birdie, go out with Mr. Durgan and wait. You cannot be afraid to leave me while he is near."

"I will not! I will not!" cried the younger, with more vehemence than seemed necessary. So excited was she that she stamped her foot as she spoke.

The tension was relieved by what seemed propriety on the stranger's part.

"I'll go away, then," he said. "I don't want to make the young lady cry. I sha'n't make you any trouble, ladies." He backed out to where Durgan stood on the verandah.

"Wait, I'll give you something," said Miss Smith. "You ought to have good food." She went to her desk, and came out giving him a folded bank-note.

"Thank you, ma'am. Good day." He went on a few steps and looked back, as if expecting Durgan to conduct him off the premises.

"I'd be much obliged, sir, if you'd show me the short way—I'm weak, sir."

Durgan indicated the trail, and followed to make sure that the negro did not return through the bushes.

As they went, Durgan saw him unfold the bank-note and take from inside a slip of written paper.

The mulatto went steadily down the mountain, without so much as looking at the kitchen door, whence Eve was regarding him with eager interest.

Adam had been in the meadow at the time of this incident. When going down to the post-office on his regular evening errand, he stopped to ask Durgan if the "yaller boy" had any genuine errand. And on the way up he stopped again, with trouble in his eyes, to give the information that 'Dolphus was spending the night there, and had suggested staying in this salubrious spot for his health.

Durgan discovered that Adam and his own negro labourers regarded the sickly and tawdry New Yorker as a peculiarly handsome specimen of their race—quite the gentleman, and irresistibly attractive to any negress—and that they agreed in denouncing his looks and manners

solely on account of the possibly vagrant affections of their own women.

Durgan believed the stranger's errand to be
purely mercenary, and feared that he was levying
some sort of blackmail on Miss Smith. He
feared, too, that Eve was abetting.

CHAPTER XII

NEXT morning Bertha rode down to the village. Later, Durgan heard that she had visited 'Dolphus, taken pains to get him a more comfortable lodging, and left him a basket of sundry nourishing foods. More than this, she had sat and talked with him in a friendly way for quite an hour. When she passed up the hill again, Durgan observed that she appeared calm and contented. She stopped to give him an invitation.

"My sister requires your attendance at supper o'clock this evening—no excuse accepted."

"Why *this* evening?" he asked.

"For two reasons. First, we are very grateful for your kindness yesterday, and sister wanted to 'make up.' Secondly, she was making your favourite chicken salad. Perhaps you think that is all one reason, but the second part makes your acceptance imperative, as the salad will be already made."

At sundown Durgan surrendered himself to the attractions of the gracious sisters and the delicacies of their table.

When Adam and his wife had been dismissed, and the three were sitting on the darkling verandah, watching the vermilion west, Miss Smith reminded them that she had the bread to "set" for next day. Bertha and Durgan were playing cards. She went through the dining-room to the kitchen at the back of the house. She was not gone long, barely half an hour; the sky had scarcely faded and the lamp but just been lit, when she came back calm and gentle as ever.

Durgan was not calm. He felt his hand tremble as he brought from the shelf a book which Bertha had asked for.

Ten minutes before a contention had arisen between himself and Bertha as to the time of the moon's rising. To satisfy himself he had walked on the soft grass as far as the gable of the house nearest his footpath. Watching a moment in the shadow, he had heard a movement in the wood. As the first moon-rays lit the gloom he saw the figure of a woman standing on the low bough of an old oak and reaching a long arm toward an upper branch. All the oaks here

were stunted and easy to climb. That this was
Adam's wife he did not doubt, till, when she
had lightly jumped down, he discerned that she
was returning attended by the dogs.

Durgan went back hastily lest Bertha should
follow him. He reported only the rising of the
moon. A moment's thought convinced him that
he had been invited that evening for the purpose
of keeping Bertha from the knowledge of her
sister's excursion. No one but Miss Smith could
have taken the dogs. He guessed that she had
fulfilled some promise to the boy, 'Dolphus—
some promise given him on the slip of paper
in the bank-note, of putting money where he
might seek it. Amazing as the method resorted
to was, Durgan felt no doubt that Miss Smith's
action was wise and right in her own eyes, but
he was convinced that she was putting herself in
danger.

He lingered a little while, not knowing what
to do. Then he spoke of 'Dolphus, taking
occasion to explain the extreme distrust he felt
concerning the man and the degraded nature
which so many of this class had exhibited.

Both sisters seemed interested, but not greatly.

"Of course, we never thought whether we
liked or disliked him," cried Bertha. "That is

not the way one thinks of men like that. We
knew him to have been unfortunate ; and he is
certainly very ill."

.Miss Smith said, with a kind smile lighting
up her face : " I think, Mr. Durgan, you don't
mean that even a 'thieving yellow nigger' hasn't an
immortal soul. Even if we can't get real religion
into his mind, we can show him kindness which
must help him to believe in the mercy of God—
not " (she added in humble haste) " that I have
ever been kind to him, but I guess Birdie tried
to be this morning."

Durgan was never far from the thought that
the slave-owning race were responsible for the
very existence of a people who had been nourished
and multiplied in their homes for the sake of
gain.

" Not only for the soul he has, but for the
diseased body of him, for all that he suffers
and for all the injury he does—he and all his
class——" Durgan stopped. Both women were
looking at him inquiringly. "Before God I
take my share of the blame and shame of it.
But it is one thing to be guilty, and another
to know how to make reparation. Take an
illustration from the brood of snakes in the
cliff here. In some slight way you are responsible

even for their existence, for you ought to have had the parents killed. But you cannot benefit this brood by kindness; you would wrong the world by protecting them. Believe me, I have been reared among these people; I know the good and bad of them; a rattlesnake is less dangerous than a man like this 'Dolphus. While I would defend such fellows as Adam with my life, if need be, I believe that I should do the best thing for the world in killing such creatures as 'Dolphus and Adam's wife. While such as I ought to bear the punishment of their sins and our own in the next world, the best reparation we could make in this would be to slaughter them."

Bertha had listened, fascinated by his most unusual earnestness of manner. But at the last words she rose hastily and went out with averted face. The tardy moon was now high. They saw her pacing the walk between the tall sides of the garden beds.

Miss Smith watched her a moment with eyes of loving solicitude, then said, " I'm sure you think you're speaking right down truth, Mr. Durgan, but, you see, *I'm* a Christian, and I b'lieve the Lord Jesus died for 'Dolphus and Eve, and not for rattlers. That makes all the difference."

"And yet it is a fact that, among the men and women for whom He died, there are fires of evil which can only burn themselves out."

"All things are possible with God," said she.

He made no reply. He was always impressed by the spiritual strength of this delicate woman. After a moment's pause it occurred to him to ask simply—

"What is your sister frightened of—I mean at different times? She seems to suffer from fears."

Slowly she raised her faded blue eyes to him with a look of deep sorrow and puzzled inquiry. "I don't know. She won't talk to me about it—Bertha won't."

"But surely——"

"Yes, I ought to know all she thinks, and be able to help her. Perhaps I know there may be something I won't admit to myself. But, Mr. Durgan, I'm real glad if she talks to you, for it's bad for her to be so lonesome. She had a great shock once, Bertha had. If you can make her talk to you, it'll do her good, Mr. Durgan."

Durgan obediently went out, and walked a few minutes with Bertha in the further shadow of the garden.

"Why did you say it ?" she asked. "How could you talk of it being good to kill anyone ?"

"My child!" he exclaimed, and then, more calmly, "you know well what I meant. We all know perfectly that there is a leprosy of soul as well as of body, for which on this side death we see no cure, of which even God must see that the world would be well rid. We cannot act on our belief; we leave it in His hands."

"Don't say it! Don't even hint at such a thing again!" In a moment she exclaimed, in a voice of tears; "What does God care? Ah me! when I look back and see my childhood—such high hope, such trustful prayer! Who gave that heart of hope but the God of whom you speak? Who taught the little soul the courage to trust and pray? And the hope is dead, the courage crushed, the prayers—may my worst enemy be saved from such answer, if answer there is, to prayer!"

She leaned her head against a tree, sobbing bitterly.

He supposed that 'Dolphus, bringing memories of a previous time, had unnerved her.

"You had a happy childhood." He spoke soothingly, hardly with interrogation.

She looked up fiercely. "You call God a

father! It was my father who taught me to pray. He—ah! you cannot think how beautiful he was, how loving, how fond of all beautiful things! He taught me to pray for him. He said that he could not pray for himself—that he had no faith. I knelt by his knee every day, and prayed, as he taught me, for him and for sister and for myself, but most of all for him. Then Hermie became religious—dear, gentle, self-denying sister—and I cannot doubt that she spent half her time in prayer for him because he wasn't converted."

"And he died?" asked Durgan.

"Yes; he died." It seemed to him that she shuddered.

"Had you ever anything to do with people who believe that the dead can return to speak to us, or appear to us?"

She raised her head and looked at him with interest.

"I once knew a man," continued Durgan, "who believed in such things, who saw such visions."

"Do you mean the man called Charlton Beardsley?"

Durgan was much surprised by hearing the name of his wife's protégé from such a source.

"I should not have supposed that you had ever even heard his name. When he came to this country you must have been at school."

"I had just left school. Tell me what he was like. Was he bad or good ?"

"I thought him simple, and much mistaken."

"Was he a wicked man ?"

"I did not think him so then; I have not seen him since."

"He lives with Mrs. Durgan now, and is a great invalid. Surely you must know if he is a wicked man ?"

"Was it the Blounts who told you about him ?"

"Yes—Mr. Blount mentioned it before you came"—he thought her words came with hesitation—"but I have wanted to ask you. He was called a mesmerist too—do you believe that one man's will could possess another person, and make that person do—well, any wicked thing ?"

"There was some talk about what was called 'mesmerism' among Beardsley's followers. He had nothing to do with it, I think. I do not believe in one man controlling another to the extent you speak of. If it can happen, it is so rare as not to be worth thought."

She sat silently thinking.

And he was egotistic enough to suppose that the unkindness of mentioning his wife might now occur to her! But when she spoke again he saw that she was only absorbed in her own thoughts.

"I suppose you are right." She sighed.

He said, "I am surprised to find your former life and mine have ever touched so nearly as that we should have taken interest in the same man. He was not a public medium—only known to a very few people. I spoke of his seeing ghosts only because I wanted an opportunity to ask you if you were frightened of ghosts."

"Oh no; I am not. I have been better taught than that. Why should you ask?"

"I see I should be ashamed of asking such a question."

"Ah! I understand. I talk so wildly at times, I have been so foolishly, childishly talkative, that you think me capable of any folly. You cannot despise me as I despise myself; but—oh, Mr. Durgan—at times I am very unhappy. If I were not terribly afraid to die, my greatest fear would sometimes be that I should live another day. It is not melodrama; it is not hysterics; it is the plain, sober truth; but I am sorry that I have let you know it."

Then, saying good night, she added, "I have the best sister in the world. I want to live bravely and be happy for her sake ; and you can best help me by forgetting what I have said and done. I had the best father in the world : by the memory of your lost daughter, help me to be worthy of him."

CHAPTER XIII

WHEN Durgan had said good night to the sisters, he made the warm moonlight night an excuse for wandering. He sat down a little way off, able to watch the lights in the house, and also the stunted oak into whose keeping he had seen Miss Smith confide something. He felt pretty sure that, as soon as the house was shut up for the night, the dogs as usual within, 'Dolphus would appear to take money from the tree.

The house was closed; the curtained windows ceased to glow; but no one climbed the tree.

The oaks were on rocky, windy ground, the old trees gnarled and conspicuous above the denser growth of low shrub. The thought of spying on any of Miss Smith's plans was revolting; his only wish was to see that the negro did not approach the house. He felt at last compelled to descend to this tree, to be sure that no one lurked near it. He had marked it by a

peculiar fork in its upper part, but he lost sight
of this fork on entering the thin wood, and
moved about carefully for some time before he
found it, and then no one was to be seen. He
stood nonplussed, wondering how long he ought
to guard the house.

The white light fell on the small leaves and
the grey moss and lichen which covered the oak
branches. It cast sharp interlacing shadows
beneath. The under thicket was of those small,
aromatic azaleas which can put forth their modest
pink and white blossoms in sterile places. To
these bushes has been given a rare, sweet scent, to
console them for lack of splendour. Durgan's
senses were lulled by this scent, by the soft air
and glamour of light. He stood a long while,
not unwillingly, intent upon every sight and
sound. No hint of any human presence came
near him.

It seemed to him at length that he heard steps
a long way down the hill on the cart-road. He
thought he heard voices.

Now he felt sure the negro was coming, and he
was exceedingly angry to believe that Eve was
with him. Who else could be there? He
shuddered to think that this false, soulless
creature knew every door and window in the

H

house, every soft place in the hearts of her mistresses, perhaps every fear they entertained. With her to help, and with some prior knowledge of the sisters' secret as the basis of his operations, what tortures might not this villain inflict, what robbery might he not commit, without fear of accusation ?   Durgan felt angry with Eve ; the other only roused his contempt. With real rage, a passion strong in his Southern nature, he slipped silently out, ready to confront the two.

But now again there was silence. He could hear nothing. At every turn the lone beauty of the place met him like a benediction. He waited. There was nothing—no one.

Then—ah, what was that sound ? what could it be—like a gasp or sigh, far away or near ? One soft but terrible sob. That was all ; but Durgan felt his spirit quail. His rage was gone ; he did not notice its absence.

The moments in which he listened seemed long, but almost instantly he found himself wondering if he had really heard anything at all. He went as quickly and quietly as he could, by the trail and the mine, to the road below, and saw 'Dolphus some way beneath, walking slowly, not up but down the road.   The casual aspect of his figure, the slight consumptive cough, effaced the weird sensation of a minute before.

" Hi ! " cried Durgan.

Bertha's terriers in the barn barked cheerfully in answer to his well-known voice. The mountain echoed a moment.

'Dolphus stood, hat in hand. A fit of coughing seized him. Durgan went down the road.

" What are you doing here ? "

" Trapping for coon, sir."

" Not coon."

" Yes, sir ; I was prospecting for a likely place to set a trap. The gentleman I've been servant to, wrote and said he'd pay me for coon skins."

" You lie."

" Yes, sir."

He stood still submissively. The full light of the moon fell on him between the shadows of the high and drooping trees. The dust of the road absorbed and partly returned the pearly light. The sylvan beauty of this sheltered bank was all around. What a sorry and absurd figure the mulatto made ! His silky hair, parted in the middle and much oiled, received also the glint of the moon. His long side whiskers hung to his shoulders ; his false jewellery flashed. This man, whose shirt-fronts and manners were already the envy of darkydom in Deer Cove, looked indeed so pitiful an object in these rich surroundings, that Durgan felt that he had overrated his power for mischief.

"I said you lied. What do you mean by saying 'yes'?"

"I would not contradict you, sir. Reckon I lied. I'm a dying man, sir; you could knock me down with a straw, sir."

"What are you doing here?"

"I came to do a service for Miss Smith. She's a holy one, sir. When I found I wasn't long to live, I thought I oughter serve her if I could."

"Serve her? You are trying some sort of trick to get money."

"Miss Smith'll see that I'm comfortable as long as I live, sir. That's all I want."

"You're trying some game to enrich yourself, and you've got Adam's wife helping you."

'Dolphus laughed out; it was a weak, hysterical giggle. "Beg pardon, sir, but the woman ain't in it. Beg pardon, I can't help laughing, sir. Reckon good, religious ladies would be a sight better off without that thieving yaller girl waiting on them."

He laughed weakly till he coughed again.

Durgan, revolted beyond measure, swore within himself that Eve should never pollute the house of the sisters by entering it again.

"Get home. Get out of my sight. If you come out here again, I'll have the General turn you out of the district."

He spoke as to a dog, but the dog did not turn and run. He leaned against a tree out of sheer weakness, but faced his enemy steadily.

"No, sir; you can't frighten me, 'cause I'm a dying man, anyway. Miss Smith, she'll speak to the General, and to the Almighty too, for me. I'll die easier 'cause I know she will." His voice had grown thin, and now vibrated with excitement. "I've just got one thing more to say, sir. You'll see I'm not frightened of you when I say it. If you knew the sort o' wife you've got, sir, and what she's been hiding, you'd look after her better than you do; and if you value your salvation, you'll stand by the pious little lady on the hill; you'll be happier when you come to die."

"Look here, my good fellow; you're very ill, I see; you're delirious. Go home and get to bed."

"Yes, sir, I'll go. But study on what I've said, sir; for it's gospel truth, as I'm a dying man."

"Can you manage to go alone? Shall I wake Adam to help you home?"

'Dolphus laughed again. "No, don't wake Adam, sir. I'll go safer alone."

Durgan, now convinced that hectic fever had produced delirium, went as far as Adam's cabin to consult him. To his surprise, he found it empty.

CHAPTER XIV

WHEN the next day was breaking, Durgan wakened to the sound of footsteps and loud lamenting. Adam, weeping like a heart-broken schoolboy, in terrified haste stumbled into the door of the hut.

"Marse Neil, suh, I've been huntin' her the whole night long, an' I've found her done dead. Marsa, come, for de good Lord's sake! She's lying all by herself on de ground. Oh, oh, my poor gal; my pore honey!"

He was now running away again, and Durgan was following. In the thick of the forest, in a hollow of coarse fern, lay the pretty Eve—a bronze figure of exquisite workmanship. One small dark wound was seen above her heart, where the torn muslin of her bodice revealed the beautiful rounding of neck and breast. She lay with her face upturned and death's seal of peace upon her lips. Big Adam knelt sobbing by her side, trying to close the fringed eyelids, which

allowed one crescent line of the velvet eye to be
seen.

"Adam, tell me what you know." Durgan's
imperious tone was a needed tonic.

The big negro drew himself up and controlled
his sobs. With a gesture towards the dead of
great simplicity he said, "I know nuthin', marsa
—nuthin' but this! Miss Smith, she sen' me
last night with a lettah for the Gen'ral. The
hoss los' a shoe, so I leave him an' walk. I
come home very late, near middle of night, an' I
meet that yaller boy, all up an' dressed, in the
Cove. So I run home, an' my poor gal was
gone from the cabin. I'se been lookin' for her
the whole night through till I foun' her. Oh,
oh! Marse Neil! my pore, pore gal!" He
broke down again in tears, casting himself beside
the corpse on the ground.

Durgan looked at the two with indescribable
sorrow. How he had desired to have this
woman out of the way—Adam free from his
thraldom, the sisters from her mischief-making!
Now! There is naught on earth can grieve the
heart of the living like the face of the dead.

The dawn brightened; the birds sang pæans
of joy; the gay wind danced; and over the
woman who had been so light and winsome a

part of yesterday's life a rigid chill had crept, which made her to-day a part only of the dark cold earth. Durgan stood with head bowed. He remembered the day his father had bought her, a babe with her mother, to save them from darker fate. In this dead body was the blood of fathers who, calling themselves American gentlemen, had, one generation after another, sold their own children as slaves. What chance had she to have in her nerve or fibre that could vibrate to any sense of good? If her spirit had now passed to plead at the bar of some great judgment-hall, on whose head must the doom of her transgressions fall?

Good!

At length he knelt on one knee and laid his hand on Adam's head. "Don't cry so! Oh, Adam; you've got your old master's son to love, you big nigger. I couldn't do without you. You'll kill yourself crying for the poor girl like that."

Adam struggled like a manful child, and subdued his grief in order to show how deep was his gratitude for this kindness.

"We were both reared in the same old place, Adam. You'll not forget that I'm lonely in the world now, too, and a poor working man like yourself—oh, Adam!"

Adam rose up. "This nigger will try and bear up an' not shame you, Marse Neil. This nigger will never forget your kindness this day, Marse Neil, suh."

Since seeing that the woman was dead, Durgan had assumed that the low soft sob which had chilled his heart the night before was nothing more than Eve's death groan. It seemed apparent that she had been stabbed to the heart too suddenly to have had more than a moment's consciousness of death. He supposed that 'Dolphus had perhaps been watched and waylaid by Eve, and in a half-delirious moment had thus disposed of her to avoid sharing the money he was seeking.

Durgan took his bearing to find out where he now was, and climbed to catch sight of the tree by which he had watched the evening before. But as soon as he could see the upper part of the hill he perceived that it was by no means sure such a sound could have been heard so far. This annoyed him, as he wished to send his testimony at once to the magistrate at Hilyard. When he remembered how 'Dolphus had laughed at the mention of Eve, how he had raved about his innocent intentions, and even ventured to slander Mrs. Durgan, of whose existence it would seem he could only know through Eve's gossip, Durgan felt persuaded of his dangerous mental state, and that there was no safety for the community till this poor irresponsible creature was in confinement. The cool daring of offering advice on his own domestic affairs was what, above all, convinced Durgan of his delirious condition.

He wrote a statement for the magistrate, giving such evidence as he could, and his belief that 'Dolphus was the only person within reach of the place where the crime was committed.

Leaving Adam to watch beside his dead, Durgan went himself to Deer Cove, sent one of his labourers to Hilyard and the other to the Blounts, set a guard over the house where 'Dolphus slept, and roused the village to Adam's aid.

It was not until he had done all he could in the interests of justice and humanity, and was again returning to his solitary hut, that it struck him for the first time how strange it was that this sorrowful thing should occur within the radius of Bertha's unaccountable terrors, that a cruel, crafty stroke, such as she would appear to dread, had actually been struck within the purlieus of her hiding-place.

CHAPTER XV

WHEN Durgan reached the stone platform of the mine, Bertha came out to meet him. She had apparently been sitting alone on some rock in the lateral cutting. She was dressed for riding; her face was quite pale, and had a strength and sternness in it that alarmed him.

"I must go at once to Hilyard. I have come to—have you not heard?"

"'Tis an affair of niggers," said he; "they are always knifing one another."

"Oh no, no! Do you not understand at all? Whom do you suppose to be guilty?"

"'Dolphus—of course."

"Mr. Durgan, for the sake of all that is true and just, and for our sakes, if you will, do not breathe such a thought to anyone. What has happened is, perhaps, what I have feared for years—what I have laboured for years to prevent. May God forgive me if I have risked too much. But the worst thing that can be done—the worst for us—would be to accuse *him*."

"My dear Miss Bertha, you cannot possibly have anything to do with this sad affair ?"

"Oh! you do not know! you do not know! Do not contradict me. Only believe me that there is more in this than you know. I fear I have done a terrible wrong in concealment, but I did it for the best. I hoped——"

"I am quite sure that 'Dolphus killed the woman."

"No. No. Alas! I am afraid I know too well who did. And I am so far yet from knowing what I ought to do that I dare not tell you more. I'm afraid that I should say too much or too little. But if you will do what I ask, I think no harm will come if I go to Hilyard without saying more than this."

"Tell me why you are going to Hilyard."

"I'm going to telegraph for our lawyer, Mr. Alden. He must come at once. I intend to say in Deer that I am going to fetch Adam's mother, who lives there; but I am really going for the other purpose."

"I cannot endure that you should mix yourself up in this affair! I am sure 'Dolphus did it. I caught him near the spot. He is very ill;

he was raving with fever, I think. But I will not argue with you. The ride may do you good."

"Will you do what I am going to ask?"

"Tell me what it is."

She had schooled herself to rapid work and action; her thought was quite clear. "I want you to be kind enough to saddle my horse and bring him down to me. I want you to explain to my sister that I have no time to go back to the house, and to tell her that there is no woman who can come to work for us to-day. I want you to speak very gently to her, for she is so distressed; but you must not tell her that I spoke of the lawyer. And first, and last, and above all, Mr. Durgan, I want you to be on your guard against an enemy. Going up to our house, and coming back, and wherever you are till I come home, be on your guard. If you will promise to do this you will be safe, and I can do my part with some composure."

Durgan looked at her, speechless with sheer astonishment. Manlike, he found the expense involved in bringing a notable lawyer a two days' journey, and into this desolate height, a greater proof that she had some substantial reason for alarm than any as yet offered to him.

"Promise me," she said. She was beyond all mood of tears or impatient excitement. She was only resolute.

He went up the hill to do her bidding, and at first found himself looking to right and left in the bushes before him, as he formerly looked upon the ground for snakes.

Miss Smith came into the front room at his knock. She was tremulous and tearful. After expressing his sympathy for the shock which her housemaid's sudden death must have given, he asked her if she thought Bertha well enough to ride alone.

"It sometimes does her good to have a right down long ride, doesn't it, Mr. Durgan? I don't quite understand the way she's feeling about this dreadful thing, but I guess she'll be safe enough riding. She's promised me to go to our good friend Mrs. Moore, at Hilyard. I don't see as the ride can do her any harm."

"If you think so," he said, "I'll saddle the horse."

But Miss Smith had something else to say. "Do you think Adam did it, Mr. Durgan? It seems dreadful to think such a thing of our good Adam, but I always feel that a man who can strike a woman might do almost any mean, bad thing."

Durgan felt to the full the hopelessness of explaining to a woman so ignorant of coloured folk as was Miss Smith, the kindness of Adam's discipline. He could only assure her of his present innocence.

"You don't think, Mr. Durgan, that it could have been——" Her face was very troubled.

"Yes; I suppose it was 'Dolphus," said Durgan. "I found him near the spot last night. He was delirious with fever, I think, and coughing badly. It's not safe to leave him at large. They'll give him medical attendance in jail. It's not likely he'll live to be hanged. I have sent what evidence I have against him to Hilyard; I could not do otherwise."

He said this in a tentative way, and found that Miss Smith did not share her sister's belief that 'Dolphus was not guilty. She only sighed deeply and said—

"The good Lord alone knows how to be just, Mr. Durgan; but I suppose the law comes as near it as it can."

"Have you any evidence concerning his former character?"

"No; I don't know anything about his character. I guess you've done just right, Mr. Durgan. I'm asking the Lord to make known whatever ought to be made known, and to hide whatever ought to be hidden, and to bless us all. I guess that's about the best prayer I can think of. But I don't mind telling you that 'twould be a dreadful trial to me or Birdie to be obliged to give any evidence. And I can say before God that we neither of us know anything about him that could have any bearing on this matter."

"You may depend upon me ; I'll keep you out of it if I can. It's only what happens constantly in a niggers' brawl."

His heart went out with more and more cordiality to the upright, tearful little lady, who, in the thick of troubles, seemed by her very life to point to God, as the church spire seems to point to heaven above the city's smoke.

When leading off the saddled horse, he stopped for a moment and looked back with irresistible curiosity, thinking of the conflicting aspects of the life that centred here.

The grass of the foreground lay patterned with the graceful shadows of acacia boughs. Between them he saw the low grey house, about which the luxuriance of flowers made the only confusion. Hens were pecking and dogs basking in the neat kitchen yard ; and Miss Smith, in

I

default of a servant, was quietly sweeping the kitchen porch. The place was like a dream of home. "Surely," he said to himself, "if the angel of peace could ever seek an earthly dwelling, she might well alight here and fold her wings."

He led the horse down the trail with brows knit, and in his mind the intention of further remonstrance with Bertha; but she mounted and rode away without a moment's delay.

Book II

CHAPTER XVI

THAT night Adam, who had given up his cabin to the female watchers of the dead, lay stretched at the door of Durgan's hut.

In the small hours Durgan was wakened by the negro's sighs.

"Oh, Adam. Can't you sleep?"

"Oh! Marse Neil, suh; d'you think my pore gal's in de bad place? The min'ster, he come to see me to-day, an' he said as how she was, 'cause she wasn't converted. D'you think so, suh?"

If Durgan had the modern distrust of old-fashioned preaching, he did not feel sure that he knew better than the preacher.

He lay a moment, thinking of the brightness and lightness of the creature so suddenly laid stark, trying in thought to place her spirit in any sort of angelic state. It would not do: the woman, as he knew her, refused to be content with any heaven his thought could offer. He could not conceive of any sane and wholesome spiritual condition to which the trivial, sensual soul could be adjusted.

"Oh, Adam, I don't know any better than your preacher; but I can tell you something that I suppose——"

"Yes, Marse Neil?" The tone told of a deep, sustained attention which surprised the educated man.

"I think the good Lord will take you to the good place when you die, and that——"

"Yes, but marsa, I done gone an' got religion long time ago, an' my pore gal she wer'n't ever converted."

"I was going to say that I think the Lord may let you be as near her there as you were here if you go on caring for her—which was all the distance between heaven and hell," he added within himself.

Before the dawn Durgan was again disturbed. Far off there was hint of a sound, the hoofs of several horses, perhaps—a ring, faint and far, of a bridle chain? Yes, certainly, horsemen were in the valley. Adam heard nothing but the throbs of his own heart-sorrow. Durgan listened. The road in the valley circled the mountain to Deer Cove. The sound of the horsemen was lost again almost before it was clearly heard. They were coming from Hilyard; were they coming further than the village? An hour later he heard them again: they were on the road to the mine.

Adam had fallen into the sleep of exhaustion. Durgan stood out on the road and listened and waited. Had Bertha met with some accident, and was this her escort home? Were the horsemen coming for some purpose, quite unknown to him, bearing on the mystery of the summit house? Alas! doubt as he would, he knew of one errand which these sounds might easily betoken. It was widely known that Adam had had quarrels with his wife.

Soon the men appeared. There were three constables, leading an extra horse. Durgan saw the handcuffs held by the foremost.

He ground his teeth in helpless indignation.

All the affection he felt for the home of his forefathers, all the warmth of the sights and sounds of his own joyous youth in the Durgan plantations, intensified his sentiment for the friend who still slept on, child-like, with teardrops on his cheek.

When Adam was taken, Durgan brooded over this wrong. He realised more and more that his certainty of the one man's guilt and the other's innocence was based only on his own estimate of their characters. The one was true to the core, the other false; but how to prove it?

About nine o'clock Bertha rode up. Her horse was jaded, her face worn.

"I started from Hilyard at daybreak," she said. "I loped nearly all the way."

"Did you meet the constables?"

Her reply was a monosyllable of brief distress.

"You saw Adam—had they 'Dolphus too?"

"Yes. Don't let us talk of it; I can't bear it."

She slid from her horse, grateful for respite, and Durgan, seeing her weariness, offered coffee and food.

She partook eagerly, as she had eaten little since the day before; but she seemed in no hurry to go on. Hers was a depression from which words did not come easily.

He asked if the telegram had been sent.

"Yes. Mr. Alden will be here the day after to-morrow."

"You had his answer?"

"No; but I know he will come as soon as possible. I could not decide what to say and what not, even in cypher: I only said, 'Come.'"

There was silence again, for Durgan was too

heartsore at the injustice done to Adam to think much of anything else.

At last Bertha broke out almost fiercely, "It was a glorious sunrise. I saw it as I came over the ridge. The clouds were like a meadow of flame-flower, and the purple colour ran riot upon the hills till the common comfortable sunshine flashed over and made all the world happy, looking as if life was good."

"It was not to see the sunrise that you started so early," said he.

"No, I could not rest. I was afraid, afraid that you would not believe what I said yester-day."

"What part of it?"

"About being on your guard. Indeed, indeed I beg of you—laugh if you like, but if you have any regard for me, do as I say. I only ask it until Mr. Alden comes. He will be here the day after to-morrow, I am sure. When I confess that I came so early because I was afraid that you would not take care of yourself, you will take heed, I am sure."

There was an awkward silence. She was hanging her head in shame, and seemed hardly able to find her way as she rose and groped for her bridle.

"If we are in this danger I will certainly escort you to the house."

"Yes ; you may do that."

So he led the horse under the green arches in the warm silence up to the gate where the dogs fawned on their mistress. Near the house Miss Smith came running to meet them. She embraced Bertha with motherly tenderness, asking crisp little questions about her journey and about Adam's mother.

"I am safe now," said Bertha, dismissing Durgan with thanks. She added in explanation to her sister, "I felt overdone with the heat. Mr. Durgan gave me coffee and brought me up the hill."

CHAPTER XVII

DURGAN felt very curious to know whether Theodore Alden, the well-known lawyer, would appear. He knew little about him except that his name was always in the papers in connection with the law courts, with philanthropic schemes and religious enterprise of an evangelical sort. Report said various things—that he would plead in no case in which he did not believe his cause to be right—that his integrity was in excess of his brains, and was the only argument he offered worthy of a juror's consideration—or, that the huge fees given him were often bribes to use his reputation in the service of crime, and that his diabolical cleverness was only equalled by his hypocrisy. These conflicting views partly arose from the fact that he had gained some notorious cases in the face of strong public opinion, and in one case, at least, it seemed against all the weight of evidence.

Whatever Alden's character, it was certain that

his hands would at any time be more than full of affairs. Bertha had only given him half a day and a night in which to prepare for the journey. Durgan had no sanguine hope of having his curiosity satisfied as soon as she expected.

Yet on the very next day, at evening, some twenty hours before the time Bertha had set, a carriage from Hilyard drove up, and while the horses were resting, a dapper, townbred Northener jumped out to inspect his surroundings.

The stranger was about sixty years of age. He had a pale face, a trim grey beard, a brisk manner, a fineness of dress, which all carried a whiff of New York atmosphere into the lateral mica cutting, which was as yet but a shallow cave. As soon as he perceived the nature of Durgan's work, he took an almost exhaustive interest in mica, although it was probable that he had never even thought of the product in its rough state before.

In vain Durgan tried to discern solicitude or impatience in the face of the stranger. He had no doubt heard of the deed with which the county was ringing, on his way from Hilyard, but that could hardly have put his mind at rest concerning Bertha's enigmatical telegram.

When the horses were ready, the traveller and

his luggage went on. The carriage soon returned empty. Durgan heard no more till the next day.

He had prevailed upon the old General to ride to Hilyard to try to obtain Adam's release, and after waiting impatiently for the result, heard by a messenger late that evening that Adam must abide his trial. Durgan was proportionately angry and distressed.

In this mood Bertha found him the morning after the lawyer arrived. She was somewhat less troubled than on the last occasion, but showed confusion in explaining her errand. She said that Alden was coming at once to see Durgan.

She added, " When I sent for him, and was so terribly frightened, I—I thought I could tell him all that I feared."

" It matters less that you should tell him what you fear, but you must tell him all that you know."

" Oh, Mr. Durgan, that is just what I cannot do—now that he is here."

" You must. One innocent man, at least, is most falsely accused. Do you think poor Adam is not made of the same flesh as you are? Think of the agony of being accused of killing one whom you fondly loved, whom you were bound to pro-

tect. Even if he is not hanged, every hour
that he lies in jail is unutterable misery to
him."

"Alas! who can know that better than I?"
she asked.

There was conviction in her tone. She raised
her face to his; then suddenly flushed and
covered it with her hands. "You don't know?
We thought you must have guessed; but Mr.
Alden will tell you. Oh, Mr. Durgan, try to
think of us as we are, not as the world thinks,
and—there! he is coming."

They listened a moment to approaching footsteps.

Bertha took hold of Durgan's sleeve in her
intensity. "Don't tell him anything I have
said," she whispered.

"Child!" he said a little sharply, "I must."

Her intensity grew. "For Hermie's sake,
don't. I will do anything you tell me in defence
of Adam. I will—yes, I promise—I will tell
you all I know, all I fear, only promise me this."
She was clinging to his arm in tears.

He gave a promise grudgingly. "Not before
I see you again, then."

"In spite of whatever he may tell you?"

"I have promised," he said with displeasure.

She had gone on, and the lawyer tripped jauntily down the path. He brought with him the suggestion of hope. He presented his card with an almost quaint formality. His manner was old-fashioned. He admired the superb view, paid a few compliments to old Georgian families and to the Durgans in particular, and apologised for his unceremonious intrusion the previous evening. He went on, in elegant and precise diction, to say that he understood from his clients at the summit house that Durgan could give him details concerning the recent deplorable death of a coloured woman who had been in their employment.

Durgan conducted him to the place where Eve was found, and to Adam's now empty cabin. They discussed the facts that no knife had been found, that the fern had taken no print of feet. Then Durgan described his first sight of 'Dolphus and the interview. He was growing very tired of a statement he had already been obliged to make more than once.

Alden took notes and gave no sign of opinion.

"The mulatto did it," said Durgan sternly.

"Very probably, my dear sir; but there is as yet no proof. In such a place, whoever did it could throw the knife where it would remain hidden for ever. There is no proof that this mulatto committed the deed before he went down the mountain; none that Adam did not do it when he returned later."

"Adam is a better man than I am. I am as certain of him as of myself."

"I entirely take your word for it. I am convinced by what you say. But men of the law, my dear sir, think only of what will convince the men in the box."

Having told all this of his own accord, Durgan became aware that in the course of conversation he was being questioned, and very closely.

Where had he gone when he left the sisters? How long had he rested? Where did he go then? Why did he wait? Did he remember exactly the place in which he waited? None of these questions were asked in categorical form, yet he had soon rather reluctantly told his every movement, except what he had seen of Miss Smith's actions when the moon rose, and the location of the particular tree. He was wholly determined that what he had so unexpectedly spied should never pass his lips.

"You were very kind in guarding the house. This coloured man was evidently a dangerous character. You had reason, no doubt, for suspecting that he would be about at that hour, Mr. Durgan ?"

"I knew nothing about his movements. I can tell you nothing more."

"Can you be sure that he made no attempt to enter the house that evening ?"

"He could hardly have done that."

"You were in the house all the evening, and then watched it till you heard the alarming sound of this poor woman's last breath. You are sure that he did not come or go from the house in that time ?"

"Have you any reason to suppose he did ?"

"Suppose, merely for the sake of argument, that I had reason to suspect he did, can you deny it ?"

"I am sure he did not."

"Could you swear to it in a court of justice ?"

"No. It was impossible for me to watch every door. I expected him from one direction, and watched only that. I should have expected the dogs to bark if he came within the paling."

"Ah! Then you could not swear that anyone who could silence the dogs might not have left the house." The lawyer relapsed into significant silence.

K

CHAPTER XVIII

AT last Alden said, "Mr. Durgan, I came here this morning at the request of my clients and dear friends to make a communication to you. When I have made it you will understand why I should have been glad had you been certain that during the evening no one could have left or entered the house—this negro or any other person. Have you any idea of what I am going to tell you?"

"I am aware that these ladies are, for some good reason, hiding. This information came to me by accident. The secret is safe with me. I have no wish to know more."

"No doubt it is safe, and we are happy that it should be in your keeping. May I ask if you came to guess it solely from those letters which this unhappy pair opened; or did any other circumstance—— ?"

"Solely through that accident."

"You feel convinced that this knowledge was only shared by these two ?"

"I quite think so. Adam will never tell ; he is as safe as I am."

"And the woman is dead."

For the first time Durgan put the two circumstances together. He felt vexed.

"You will naturally suppose," said Alden, "that when Adam is tried, my clients will go into court and give evidence as to his excellent character. But if it is possible to prevent it, they must not do that. It was never by my advice that they secluded themselves and took an assumed name ; it was Bertha who insisted on seclusion. I would have preferred that they had had strength to live in the open. I should not have greatly cared had all the country found out who they were, but for this crime, which is the most unfortunate that could have happened at their doors. Their identity must now be hid, if it is possible without wickedness."

Durgan had been trying jealously to find some element of falsity beneath the Northerner's quiet face and dapper exterior. Now he no longer doubted his sincerity. The lawyer sat looking absently down where the beautiful valley lay in all its summer tranquillity, framed in the peace of the eternal hills, and Durgan saw the beads of sweat break upon his brow. He was convinced that he had more than the interest of clients at stake, that his whole heart was in some way concerned in this matter.

Alden spoke slowly. "I have known these women since Bertha was a mere girl. Eight years ago I was working in the same mission school with the elder sister. For three years we met twice a week, with the most sacred of all interests in common. Constantly I had the pleasure of walking to or fro with her, and we talked together on the great theme of religion. After that I knew her intimately in the midst of the greatest of sorrows a woman could endure. I have strengthened our friendship by every means in my power ever since. Is it possible that I could be mistaken in her character?"

His small blue eyes had grown deeper and bluer as he spoke; the lines about them also deepened. Sorrow, and that of the nobler sort, was written there. Durgan liked him.

"I am sure that our friend is a true woman," said he.

"And yet," Mr. Durgan, "she is publicly believed to have committed the most barbarous of crimes. She is Hermione Claxton."

Durgan uttered an exclamation of dismay. The two men turned from each other with mute accord.

To Durgan it seemed strange and terrible that here, in these splendid mountain solitudes, the edge of such a shameful thing should enter his own life. Below the rock, the forest in glossy leaf breathed in the perfect sunlight; rank below rank stood shining trees like angelic hosts in pictures of heaven. The air was filled with the lullaby of unseen herd-bells. Afar, where the valley widened and purpled, the mountain stream, in quiet waters, was descried, and sunny fields.

Before Durgan's mind lay the daily papers of the time of the notorious trial of Hermione Claxton—the sensational headlines, the discursive leaders. In his ears echoed the universal conversation of that time—voices in tramcars, public-houses, and streets. The natural horror of brutal deeds, which had made him recoil then, darkened his outlook now like a cloud. But in the midst of this obscurity upon all things two figures stood, a moving vision—Bertha, fresh and beautiful, faulty and lovable, and beside her the fragile sister, grey-haired and upright, with steadfast face turned heavenward.

Alden spoke first. "You are aware, Mr.

Durgan, that Mr. Claxton and his second wife were suddenly killed, that a large body of circumstantial evidence proved that Hermione was alone in the house with them, that by her own arranging she was alone with them—in fact, I must say there was complete circumstantial proof that she had committed the heinous crime. There was even motive, if just anger and love of money are motive enough. Against this stood, I may say, only her personality, for so reticent and modest is she that few knew her character. To my mind it is a great honour to America that the twelve ordinary men who formed the jury could be so impressed by her personality that, while the whole world hooted, they were resolute in a verdict of acquittal."

"It was you—your eloquence that did it."

"So the world said : but I only appealed to their sense of truth, and out of the truth of their hearts they pronounced her ' not guilty.' You are aware, Mr. Durgan, that the world pronounced another verdict."

Durgan would have been glad to be silent. In the rush of his thought he was conscious that he chose the most childish thing to say. "But —but—someone must have done it."

When Alden did not seem to find this remark

worthy even of assent he hastened, stumbling, to explain it. " I would be understood to mean that, familiar as you were with them, it is hardly possible that you do not suspect, do not, perhaps, know, who might be guilty. I am not, of course, asking you who—I have not the slightest right to ask—but——"

" Do you suggest that, while the whole nation was roused, and rightly, to demand justice, I screened the sinner ?. Mr. Durgan, I come of Puritan descent. So strongly do I feel the wickedness of lax justice that if my own son had done it I would have led him to the scaffold."

Durgan believed him. There had flashed out of this little dainty man so hot a spark from the lightnings of Mount Sinai that the onlooker felt for the moment scorched by the sudden heat.

Also by this time Durgan had perceived that his imputation had really arisen, not from the public reports of the case, or from Alden's epitome, but from his knowledge of Bertha's perplexity, terror, and distress. He was glad that Alden went on without waiting for reply.

" You must surely be aware, Mr. Durgan, that, admitting the daughter's innocence, the case was one of those termed ' mysteries,' and ranks among the most obscure of these. The murder must have been the work of some maniac intruder; my own suspicions have always centred about a boy who certainly came to the house that morning, but was never heard of after, although large rewards were offered. But that only shifts the unknown a step further back. Who was this boy who could so vanish? Who sent him, and who concealed him? Indeed, Mr. Durgan, who can have thought on this problem as I have done? And there were many even astute lawyers and commercial men who have confessed to me that they induced insomnia by merely trying to conceive an adequate explanation. Remember that the dual crime and the vanishing of this boy occurred at midday in a fashionable neighbourhood in a household noted for propriety, elegance, and culture. I, who know more than anyone else, know nothing; but this I do say, Mr. Durgan: rather than believe Hermione Claxton guilty, I would believe that the deed was done by an invisible fiend from the nether world; and I am not superstitious."

"I quite agree with you. Anyone who knows Miss Claxton must agree with you. She is innocent of every evil thought."

But he felt that he spoke mechanically. His mind was turning with more and more distress and bewilderment to Bertha's talk and behaviour. He was glad when Alden went away for the time, although he knew that the question of Adam's defence must be quickly settled.

Alden left him with the words : " I will come back, Mr. Durgan. You can see now that if that insane thing called the public got hold of the fact that the victim of last week's crime belonged to the Claxton household, unless it could be proved that no one issued from the house that evening——"

" I understand," Durgan answered with ill-controlled impatience.

The small man squared his shoulders and looked up staunchly. " We must save her at any cost, save that of breaking God's law."

CHAPTER XIX

THOSE elemental emotions, the protection of feebleness, the vindication of womanhood tender and motherly, were aroused in Durgan to the heat of passion. In heart he joined hands firmly with the little lawyer who had fought the battle so long. He had saved this good woman once from the worst peril, but Durgan feared there was more to come, and was panting to establish her innocence.

He struggled with a temptation. If he could swear that he had heard Eve's last breath at an hour when it was known the husband was away, this evidence would set Adam free. He believed himself to have heard it, conjecturing that either some peculiar atmospheric condition had obtained, or his senses had been strained to abnormal acuteness, or the passing spirit, terrified, had flown for safety to the nearest friend, bringing its sob of fear when it was but an instant too late to seek human aid. Why not continue to conceal the fact that he had been half a furlong beyond all natural earshot of the woman's death? He would not have known so precisely where he was had not Miss Smith's action caused him to mark one tree among its fellows. Neil Durgan, striding into court at Hilyard to give his evidence concerning the death of one of his father's slaves, was not likely to be strictly cross-questioned. The terror of the past to both sisters and Bertha's present terrors (which must yet be inquired into and allayed), surely this was enough trouble without unnecessary delay and hesitation in the course of justice at Hilyard.

Durgan was at work all day, and desired in hacking and hewing the rock to temper his own mind to meet the need of the hour, hardly knowing on which side of his path honour lay, and caring more to succeed than to be scrupulous.

While the day spent itself, his thought upon all that had occurred became clearer. It was obvious that first, before taking another step, he must know the whole warp and woof of Bertha's suspicions, which at present seemed to him so flimsy. He must know each thread, or Alden must know. At this point he stopped to marvel. On what pretext should Bertha seek to deceive so good a friend as Alden? And could it be that neither sister had confessed to Alden that the criminal had some sinister hold over them ?

Perhaps, after all, to give evidence against 'Dolphus was not the first step out of this coil of trouble. In revenge the nigger might be able to declare what they all desired most to keep silent. Bertha's strongly expressed desire in the matter strengthened this idea.

That afternoon the carriage of the Durgan Blounts was drawn by foaming thoroughbreds up the rough and winding road to the summit of Deer. Mrs. Durgan Blount was with her husband, and young Blount rode beside on his chestnut mare.

They stopped at the mica cutting to converse cheerfully with Durgan on the frequency of knifing among niggers and the obvious purpose of their journey.

The dame spoke languidly. "We thought it incumbent to offer our sympathy to the Northern ladies. This ghastly thing having happened on our property, and so close to the site these ladies have bought, we felt obliged."

"Come along, Neil Durgan," said the old General. "Jump in and call with us ; it ought to be a family affair."

Durgan excused himself, wondering grimly

what effect the name of Claxton would have had on this family expedition.

The son waited till his mother's carriage had gone on. "You are quite sure it was the yellow boy who did it? I heard at the post-office that you had found his knife."

Durgan explained that this was not so, but reiterated his conviction as to the guilt of 'Dolphus.

Said Blount slowly, "Your opinion will be conclusive. It wouldn't go far in a Northern court, perhaps; but here, and for niggers, if you tell your tale well it will prove sufficient."

"I'd be satisfied to get Adam off, if that could be done without hanging the other."

Blount stooped forward to rub the mare's ears and smooth her silken mane. His young countenance was benign and thoughtful.

"You had better have him sentenced," he said quietly. "It's annoying for you, of course, because the result rests with you—the General settled that with the judge. But it's your duty; and you do more for the world in ridding it of one villain than by a lot of charity."

Durgan felt ill-satisfied now with the sentiment of these last words, although a few days before it had been his own.

Young Blount rode away with serious mien. The hot sunflecks fell between chestnut boughs upon horse and rider and tawny wheel-ruts.

At sunset Durgan went up to the meadow, where he knew Bertha would come to feed her four-footed friends. As he waited he sat on the ledge of the wooden barn.

He saw Bertha come through the meadow gate. The calves ran to meet and conduct her to the place of feeding. Handsome young things they were, red and white, with square heads and shoulders. They formed a bodyguard on either side of the terrier and mastiff, which always had the right of place nearest to her. Thus Bertha advanced down the green-grown road between the ranks of deep, flowering grass. She carried a bucket and a basket with fine, erect balance, one in either hand.

The meadow slanted upward from the barn. As Durgan walked to meet her and take the burden, he could just see over its rise the heads of the opposite mountains. A wide gulf of slant sunbeams lay between.

Bertha greeted him with serious mien. When he had taken her load and fallen into line among her animals, she said—

"You know the worst about us now."

"Do I?" asked he. For he discovered at that moment that the question he must now put was a cruel one, and could not be shirked or smoothed over.

"Alas!" She uttered the one deprecating word slowly, and moved on in silence.

The bull calf pushed its powerful head under her hand, which now hung free, and she walked, leaning upon it, till the mastiff slowly inserted himself between the two, and, with a sudden push of its side, ousted the calf, who took a short scamper and returned head downward toward the mastiff's broad flank. The terrier laughed aloud: no one could have interpreted his snorts of delight otherwise. The mastiff reluctantly withdrew his soft nose from Bertha's palm, and attended to matters of defence. All the calves scattered in an ungainly dance, and all returned circling the dogs with lowered heads. Bertha watched these antics with a sad smile; then by sundry cuffs and pats put an end to the feud.

When they had fed the calves and the other creatures who lived in sumptuous hutches and styes behind the barn, Durgan asked his question.

CHAPTER XX

BERTHA and Durgan were standing in the broad central doorway of the barn. Hay, full of meadow flowers, was piled high to right and left. The air was full of dried pollen, and golden with the level sunlight.

"Do you know who it was that killed your parents?" Durgan asked.

She put up trembling hands in the brave pretence of shielding her eyes from the sun. Her whole body shook; her head sank on her breast.

At last she said in faint tones, "You think *this* because I warned you of danger—because of all I have said; but I was distracted, and at that time I did not foresee that you must be told who we are."

"All that is true. I am more sorry for you than words can say; but it must be better for you to share a secret you seem to be nursing alone, and you cannot think I would ask if I did not need to know."

She did not answer. He suspected that she was using all her attention to regain self-control and the strength that she had lost so suddenly.

"You told me that you thought you knew who committed this second crime," he said, "and I am convinced that you connect it with that other."

A low moan escaped her. Her head sank lower.

"I believe that the nigger is guilty, but I can't go to court and swear away his life, knowing only what you have told me and no more."

She whispered eagerly, "Will it do if I swear now that I believe I was mistaken—that I knew nothing, or, at least, no proof to the contrary?"

"Have you ever had the least reason to suppose that another person capable of these crimes lurked upon Deer?"

"If I swear to you that I never thought any-one else was near us, or on the mountain, will that satisfy you?" She was leaning her brow heavily on the hand that shaded her face.

"No one else—else than——?"

She did not help him out. She sat down, or rather crouched, on the steps of the loft.

He said very gently but resolutely, "You think, then, that your sister committed these crimes."

L

She put up her hands. "Do not, do not say it. Oh, I have never thought it possible that you could be so cruel as to say such a thing to me. Leave me in peace; for God's sake, leave me!"

"Child! even if I could leave you, it is not right that you should go on nursing this terrible suspicion alone. In the back of your mind you believe this thing, and think that some time—any time, she may repeat the crime; and the terror of it is killing you."

She was trembling violently, her face buried in her hands.

"Have you allowed anyone else to know of this suspicion of yours? Tell me, have you talked it over with a single soul?"

"No, no; oh no," she moaned. "For pity's sake, stop speaking! I never thought anyone would dare to say this to me."

"That is just what I supposed. You have nursed the idea in absolute secret. You have not even allowed your sister herself to know what you think."

"I beg that you will say no more."

"You are guarding this idea in heroic silence. You imprison it in darkness, and think it would be more terrible if you brought it out to the light. You are wrong. It will vanish away in the light. It is not true."

She started, looking up at him with wide eyes in which the tears were arrested by surprise. The flush on her face faded. She grew pale to the lips with excitement.

"How do you know?" she whispered hoarsely. "Tell me—do you know? How?"

"I know just as I know that I did not do it— or you. You did not see her do this terrible thing."

"Oh, you know nothing." She sank down again and rocked herself, moaning, "You know nothing, nothing. Why did you deceive me?"

"Tell me, then—on what grounds have you formed this belief?"

She grew more quiet, drooping before him as if in despair.

"I must go to Hilyard to-morrow. I must know first what I can say. You must tell me why you, even for one hour, believed 'Dolphus to be innocent before I go. I must judge for myself of what you tell me, but you must tell me all you know—or else you must tell Alden."

At that she uncovered her face and sought to speak calmly. "I cannot tell Mr. Alden; I beseech you, spare me that. I thought I could tell him. Then, when he came—ah, I saw then what I never knew before—that he loves Hermie—that she loves him. There is a far deeper friendship between them than I knew. I was but a girl when they used to be together, and now——

It is so sad to see the feeling he has for her. She has grown so old, and so has he—so prematurely old. This sorrow has been so deep to them both. The night that he came here he reproached her for not letting him protect her more openly. He asked her to marry him now—even now; it seems he has asked her before. Surely it must be left to her to tell him if he must ever know, if she must ever endure the anguish of his knowing."

Durgan could hardly believe his own sense of hearing, so calmly certain did she seem of the verity of her secret.

"Your sister could not tell Mr. Alden what is not true. She is wholly innocent. She can never, thank God, have any misery that accrues to one who has committed an evil deed."

"You know nothing," she repeated gently, "and oh, I am in a terrible perplexity; I do not know what to do. I am in far greater straits than you know of, Mr. Durgan. You urge me to tell you—will you accept my confession in

confidence? Otherwise—ah, if you tell Mr.
Alden what I have already said, it seems to
me that I shall die of grief and shame. I
could never look my dear sister in the face
again."

"You have no choice now but to tell me.
The life of an innocent man must be saved;
your sister's name must be kept out of the trial.
For their sakes I am bound to consult Mr.
Alden about what you have already told me,
unless, upon knowing your whole story, I think
I am justified in keeping your secret. I am
your friend. I can have no possible desire but
to serve your sister and yourself."

"But truth—justice? Would you sacrifice us
to a fetish you call 'justice,' pretending it is
God? I have always felt that you would not.
Mr. Alden would, even if it cost him his own
life."

Durgan meditated on this aspect of Alden's
character. He could perceive that from her
point of view this characteristic made him
terrible. In her trouble she had blindly put
her finger on perhaps the main difference between the virtue of the South and that of the
North.

"Hermie has always told me that about him,

but till this time I never entirely believed her. Now I do. The more he loved Hermie, the more—— Oh, Mr. Durgan, it is terrible to think of!"

He looked down pityingly. "The thoughts that you are enduring, child, are too terrible for you to bear alone. You must trust me. We Southerners were never taught to think, as the Puritans did, that the whole heart of God could be translated into a human code. I am not as good a man as Alden, but if I were——"

"Oh, I can trust you," she cried. "I know I can. And you are right—I must, I ought, to speak; but do not know how, or how much. Question me, and I will answer."

"On what possible ground can you believe this of your sister?"

"On the ground of her own confession. It is written and sealed up; I know where it is."

She had again crouched down on the lower step, and her face was hidden; but her shaken voice was quite clear and resolute.

Durgan was amazed into silence. The sun, in a dry, empty sky, had slowly descended to the dark rim of the Cherokee ridge. Now it seemed to set suddenly, and a cold shadow rose over Deer. Bertha saw nothing, but to Durgan the change in the atmosphere lent emphasis to her statement, and all the combative part of his nature rose up against it. He was convinced that there was no such confession.

CHAPTER XXI

"ARE you sure of what you tell me?" asked Durgan.

Bertha answered, "Yes; I do not know what she wrote, but I am sure it was her confession."

"You don't know what she wrote," sharply. "How do you know she confessed?"

"She told me so."

"Then, even in the face of that, I say she is innocent."

"Innocent—ah, yes indeed—of any motive, any intent, of any knowledge at the moment of what she was doing. As innocent as any angel of God. Do you think I do not know the heart, the life, of my sister? It was madness, or the possession of a demon. It was madness that came suddenly, like a fit or stroke. That is why I want to know what I ought to do. It may come back; any excitement, any association with the former attack, might bring it back. Oh, consider her case, and tell me what I ought to do. When you first came I was terrified. You did not see how much roused she was—she is so shy and quiet—but I saw a new light in her eyes. Your name is mixed up with the thought of our father in a very sad way. I was frightened then, but mercifully nothing happened. Then about the letters—ah, she was vexed about that, and I was so frightened lest she should be ill again. Then, when the coloured boy came, I dared not let her be alone with him. He brought all the details of that dreadful time back to us and—ah, I thought, living as we do and keeping him from her, I had taken every precaution, but—on the morning after that poor woman was killed, I found, oh, Mr. Durgan, I found her handkerchief in the wood where she never goes. I found it because the dogs were scenting something and I followed, and the place was in a direct line from where poor Eve——" she stopped, shuddering.

"You did not tell Alden this?"

"Oh no. How could I? And *now* I hardly believe—at least, I don't think she could have been out that night. She has been so calm since. I am sure she cannot have gone out; but I don't know—I don't know what I ought to believe or do."

The miserable recital of her fears and per-
plexities came to an end only when her voice
failed her. Durgan had been obliged to listen
attentively to gather her full purport. He knew
certainly that Miss Claxton had been out alone
that night, that the tree which she had climbed
was, in fact, in a line between Eve's beautiful
death-bed and her own back door. Nor did
anyone know at what hour Eve died. His own
assumption that Miss Claxton had gone out only
as far as the tree to leave money for 'Dolphus
had only the slightest foundation, and the
mulatto's movements certainly did not confirm it.

While he reviewed all this with some reasonable horror, he found that his inward belief of
the propriety of all Miss Claxton's actions was
not shaken. His faith was obstinate, and facts
had to be made to fit into it.

"Let us take this terrible secret of yours, and
spread it out to the light quite calmly. You
believe your sister did this first dreadful thing
in a fit of sudden madness, from which she
seems to have recovered immediately, as no one
else thought her mad. Did you believe this at
the time of the trial?"

"I did not know what to think then."

"After that, while you were abroad together, were you always in terror like this?"

"Oh no. It was when we were coming home that my sister had an illness. It was then that she told me of her confession and where to find it if it was ever needed. Then, knowing what must have been the matter, and that it might come again, I was determined to find a lonely house where I thought I should be the only one in danger. I thought I could take that risk, as I only risked myself. When we found this house I felt sure we were safe from intrusion and excitement."

"After you heard of this confession you decided that she was subject to homicidal mania. When I intruded on your privacy you feared for my life in your house. You have feared for your own life whenever any cause of excitement came up, and thought everyone near her was in danger. You think now that such an attack may have been the cause of Eve's death."

Bertha rose up in the twilight, looking like a trembling, guilty thing, and slunk away from his cool voice and overbearing manner.

"Do you think I have been so terribly wicked to keep this secret?" she moaned.

"I think you have been very foolish; but as

your folly arose from tenderness to your sister, I suppose you must be forgiven. You ought to have told your sister or Alden, or consulted a good doctor. You would have found then that you were mistaken."

"How could I speak to anyone without causing suspicion? How could I speak to her when I thought her only chance of continued health lay in forgetting? Indeed, our own family doctor, who never guessed this, told us after the trial was over that our only chance of health and leading useful lives was never to talk or let ourselves think of our trouble. Before we went abroad he warned us again and again."

"He was wise. And you—have you been obeying him?"

"How can you speak to me like this?"

"It is the medicine you need. Your sister is not mad—has never been mad. It is now years since your misfortune, and had there been want of balance or brain disease, it would have shown itself by now. Your sister is not obstinate or foolish. She is not subject to attacks of emotion, nor does she lack self-control. There is no sign of any such mania as could make such a crime possible to a well-principled woman."

"But—oh, but—I read constantly in the

papers of people who kill themselves, or kill others and themselves afterwards. The verdict is always 'temporary insanity.' I supposed there was such a thing."

"That verdict is usually a cloak for ignorance; but it assumes that had such people lived they would have shown symptoms of mental disease."

Bertha raised her hands and clasped them above her head. She drew a long breath, dilating her frame, and looked off where an empty yellow sky circled a fading landscape. "If I could only believe you—ah—if I could only believe you, I should ask no greater happiness in heaven."

"Believe me, I am telling you the truth."

"But—but——"

"Sit down again, child," he said.

The term "child," used constantly by the negroes to express half-humorous or gentle chiding, comes very naturally to Southern lips. It carried with it little suggestion of the difference of age between them, but gave a sense of comradeship and good-will which comforted her. He pulled down a bundle of hay to cushion her seat on the steps.

"Now tell me all the 'buts,'" he said.

"Alas, Mr. Durgan, you cannot scold away

our great trouble and my fears. You cannot smile them into insignificance; but now I am willing to tell you our story, and when it is told I hope you will see that you, too, must bury it for ever in silence, as I have tried to do."

She began again. "There is another reason, which you don't know yet, why I must tell you now. It is this 'Dolphus. I will try to be quick. Do you know all that was put in the newspapers about us—about the trial?"

Durgan made a sign of assent.

"Day after day the court discussed every detail of our family life and of that awful day —held it up to the whole world with an awful minuteness and intensity. And Hermie was in prison when she was not in court—oh, I wonder we lived—and it was all such a farce. They got hold of everything but the things that mattered. They never came near them.

"They tried to make out that we hated poor mamma because she was not our own mother, and were jealous lest papa should make a will in her favour. What rubbish! She was only a pretty doll, and had money of her own. No one could hate her, and papa never thought of leaving her our money. We never thought about his will."

"I quite believe that," said Durgan heartily.

"The facts they did not get hold of were about the boy they made such a mystery of."

"What did they know about the boy?"

"One of the servants let him in, and one of the neighbours saw him come in. They both took him for a beggar : one thought he was an Italian. Hermie and I knew more. I gave evidence that he had come in, and that we had not seen him leave the hall, where he waited, or seen him again that morning, which was true. But he did not come as a beggar, he did not go away before the trouble, or vanish after it. He was hidden in the house all that day, and we arranged his escape at night. In court they never asked questions that I could not answer about him, for they never once guessed."

"Guessed what?"

"That we wanted to save him. Their one idea was that we wanted him to be found. Mr. Alden moved the earth to find him, and he was conducting our case."

"Who was the boy?"

"May I tell you all I know? The boy was 'Dolphus. He was only a messenger—a servant of that man who was raising spirits in dark rooms and making them give messages and——"

"You mean Beardsley ?"

"Yes. You said the other night that he was supposed not to be a common medium. My sister has told me that Mrs. Durgan——"

"Yes, yes, I know."

"I only mean that just a few people went to him, and my father had gone. Oh, I believe he went often, and he used to tell us things that vexed Hermie so."

"What things ?"

"Oh, about knocks and tables moving. And then dear father began to receive knocks and messages from our mother. That made Hermie almost frantic. She remembered mother well, and was offended. She called it 'profanity.' But I am sure my father did not know how it vexed her ; he was always so considerate."

"The boy came from Beardsley ?"

"Oh yes. We knew, and know, nothing about the boy. He asked for my father, and was told to wait in the kitchen. I saw him there, and so did the maids. But only Hermie knew about the note—he gave it to her. She took it upstairs. I saw that she looked very white and angry. She told me that it was a message from that 'shameful impostor.' Then Hermie asked me to gather fruit in the garden, and she sent out the maids up the street. Then, some time after that, she—ah, you know it all !—gave the alarm. She called in people, and they went and rang for the police. She was very calm. Everyone knows the whole story after that."

"Yes ; but tell me what you did."

" She never allowed me to go into that room where—— She told me my father was too much disfigured for me to recognise him. Oh, I thought of nothing but the loss of my father all that day. I went into his dressing-room and cried there. I took out his dear clothes and laid my head on them. Hermie sat with me part of the day. The police were in charge of the house ; but no one had thought then of accusing her.

" When it was dark night Hermie came to me and said that there was something we could do for father's sake, and I must help her. She told me the boy was in the house and he was innocent, but that if he was found he might be arrested unjustly. She told me that some great disgrace might fall on father's name if we did not get him safely away. Oh, I did not at all understand at the time that she meant that if he were charged she must confess and be convicted. She chose some clothes of father's, and then I

M

found that the boy was locked in a very narrow press in that very room. He put on the clothes, and he and Hermie knotted some dark thing together and we let him down from the window in the dark to the garden. He got in the neighbour's garden. She told him how to get from garden to garden. The police were about, but he got away. Her mind seemed quite clear. She said that because the boy was innocent it was our duty to tell nothing that could lead to his capture. She never told Mr. Alden that she knew who the boy was or who sent him, that he had brought a letter, or how he escaped."

"But how was she so certain that he was innocent?"

"Ah, that is what I have asked myself night and day for years. What could make her certain but one thing? She *knew*, and if she knew that anyone else had committed the deed, why not tell and exonerate the boy?"

"It is most extraordinary," said Durgan. The words were wrung from him almost without his will.

Bertha took no notice. "Then that night she did not know what she was saying. She thought she saw all sorts of strange things in the room, and she talked continually, as if seeing people who were not there. Her words were quite fantastic and related to nothing I could understand. But occasionally, when she seemed more coherent, she told me that the police would come for her, that she would be proved to be guilty, and begged me in the most touching terms to love her in spite of all. In the daytime she would get up and go about the house, and she appeared composed; but I knew her well enough to see that she was still strange. But she never said a word, except when we were alone, to lead anyone to suppose that she knew more than she first told. On the third day Mr. Alden told us that she would be taken to prison. It was an awful shock to me, but it seemed to rouse her and bring back her faculties. We were alone together for about an hour. After she had tried to soothe and comfort me by speaking of duty, of God, and of heaven, she spoke to me very solemnly, and told me not to grieve for any hardship that befell her, for she had broken the law and must suffer if she was condemned; but that, short of doing or saying anything to inculpate anyone else, she would do all that could be done to convince the world of her innocence. She said, 'It would be worse for you, and for father's sake, if I were convicted.

I will fight for my liberty unless someone else is accused ; but remember, if anyone else is accused, I shall have to do what will bring disgrace. Remember that, Bertha. Remember that if any circumstance should come to your knowledge to tempt you to accuse anyone else, *that* will put an end to my hopes.' She said this very solemnly several times. Then she told me the lines on which Mr. Alden would probably have the case conducted ; and that I must tell nothing but the truth, but refuse to tell about the boy, or what she had told me. I never heard anyone speak more clearly and collectedly. She foresaw almost everything. Our other lawyers and Mr. Alden said the same thing, that her intellect was almost like that of a trained lawyer in its prevision of the effect of evidence."

" And did you believe her guilty ? "

" I did not know what to think. I was stunned. I dared not think, for it took all my mind to act the part she assigned to me. But afterwards, during the long time she was in prison and during the trial, I believed her innocent. When I thought of her goodness and the perfectly unforeseen and inexplicable manner of the way poor papa and mamma died, I could not think Hermione guilty, and I did not. As to the wild things she said in those nights, I supposed she had been in a fever, and put down all I could not understand to that.

"Then we formed the plan of going abroad and returning to some place like this, only not so lonely. We packed all our valuables to be put in a safe by Mr. Alden. When my sister had packed the family papers and her own jewelry and locked and sealed the box, she called me to look at it and gave me the key. When she was ill in Paris she told me of her confession, and that it lay at the bottom of this box. But she asked me most solemnly never to open it unless someone else was falsely accused. She told me that she had no further motive in life than to make up to me as far as possible for all that I had innocently suffered; but she begged me not to make life too hard for her by ever speaking of this matter again. I have never spoken to her again about it."

Bertha's voice had become very melancholy; now she ceased.

"This mulatto calling himself 'Dolphus is certainly the boy?"

"Yes—oh yes; we both knew him the moment he turned up again."

"Have you never seen him between then and now?"

"No."

"Where has he been?"

"I don't know."

"How did he find you?"

"By bribing the porter in Mr. Alden's office to show him the letters he carried. He has a right to protection and support from us, for there is still a great reward offered for him. Mr. Alden offered it."

"And Alden does not guess that this is he?"

"How should he? He has no idea that we would hide him. But now we cannot conceive what will happen, for although we are sure that he won't tell about us as long as he has a chance of escape, Hermie herself says that if he is condemned he may, in despair and revenge, tell all that he knows."

"Alden must be told this."

She sprang up with great energy. "He must not know. It is the one thing Hermie will not let him know if it is possible to help it. Oh, of course the worst catastrophe may come and overwhelm us; but while we have hope of escape, Hermie will not let Mr. Alden know that."

It had become dark. Hermione Claxton was looking for her sister, walking across the meadow and calling in motherly tones.

"Answer me just one thing. Did your sister tell you in plain words that she committed this deed?"

"No; she did not. But I have tried to make what she said mean anything else. In any case she would not have said a word she could help; such words are too terrible. Can you think I have not sought to believe otherwise?"

She said this in a tense, hurried voice, and standing at the barn door, called back, "I'm coming, I'm coming, dear."

"She never did it," said Durgan strongly. "She knows who did. She is shielding some-one."

"That is very easy to say," said the girl scorn-fully. "Of one thing I am certain; there is no one on earth she would shield at my expense. Think what we have suffered while she fought through that terrible trial. She knows no one, loves no one on earth, but me and Mr. Alden."

"I'm coming, I'm coming, darling."

She took up her empty pail and ran.

CHAPTER XXII

WAKING or sleeping, one figure stood forth in Durgan's imagination that night, and was the centre of all his mental activity—it was Hermione Claxton.

He had been accustomed to regard her as the very incarnation of the commonplace, in so far as good sense and good feeling can be common.

Now he knew her as the chief actor in a story wherein the heights and depths of human passion had been so displayed that it might seem impossible for one mind to habitually hold so wide a gamut of experience in its conscious memory. This quiet little grey-haired housewife, who lived beside him baking, sweeping, and sewing her placid days away, had stood in the criminal dock almost convicted of the most inhuman of crimes. Having passed through the awful white flame of public execration, she had accepted her blackened reputation with quiet dignity; for years she had lived a hidden life of perfect self-sacrifice, devoting herself to the purest service of sister love. With character still uncleared, she had been urged to take her place as the wife of one of New York's best-known philanthropists, with whom, it seemed, she had long suffered the sorrows of mutual love and disappointment. Of more than this Durgan felt assured. As he reviewed all that had been told him that day, he was the more convinced that she had been no involuntary victim of false accusation, that she knew the secret that had puzzled the world, and had chosen to shield the criminal, to bear the odium, and also inflict it on the objects of her love. She had done all this for the sake of—what? What motive could have been strong enough to induce a wise and good woman to make such a sacrifice and endure the intolerable keeping of such a secret?

Durgan very naturally sought again the bundle of criminal reports which had fallen into his hands after the fire. Packed in the pile which fed the miners' stove, they had not, as yet, been burned. He reconsidered them, supposing now that they had been collected by Miss Claxton herself. A motley band of prisoners was thus evoked. They passed in procession before Durgan, beginning with Hermione Claxton, and ending with that curious figure of the dilettante priest who had beaten a sister to death in fear that she was an apparition. The well-born woman who, without temptation, had stolen jewels, the French peasant who had killed a loved wife to save her from the sufferings of a painful disease, and all the other members of this strange procession, represented the eccentricities of the respectable, rather than the characteristics of the degraded class. From a fresh scrutiny of each Durgan gained no information, only a strong suspicion that the criminal for whom Miss Claxton had so bravely stood scapegoat belonged to the same respectable class. He assumed that while her lawyers had been hunting for some inconsequent housebreaker who had taken a maniacal delight in dealing death, she had covered the guilt of someone whose reputation defied suspicion. Love, blind love, could have been the only motive strong enough to initiate and sustain such a course of action. The only way to discover the villain to whom she had sacrificed herself was to discover the man to whom she had given her heart. No doubt, since the crime and cowardice had betrayed his true value, such a woman would turn with some affection to a man like Alden. But Durgan's surmise required that before the crime she should have had another lover. Such a lover, if at enmity with the father and in need of money, would have had all the motive that the prosecution had attributed to Miss Claxton. She was supposed to have sent all witnesses out of the house before the crime; if her lover was demanding a private interview with her father, and her engagement was as yet private, such action on her part—— But Durgan paused, vexed at the nimbleness of his fancy. He derided himself for assuming that so obvious a suspicion had not long ago been probed to the bottom by acuter minds than his.

When he came to question more soberly what clues he held by which he might himself seek for any truth in his new suspicion, more unquiet suggestions came thick and fast.

More than once lately he had had the unpleasant sensation of hearing his wife's name very unexpectedly. Bertha had more than once referred to her; and what was it the raving mulatto had said? It took him some time to recollect words that had fallen on his astonished ears only to convince him of their nonsense. The mulatto had implied that his wife had concealed something for years which put her in

172 THE EARTHLY PURGATORY

some rivalry or enmity with Miss Claxton. His
advice that Durgan should look into his wife's
conduct and take Miss Claxton's part could, if
it meant anything, only point to some mutual
interest both women had with the spiritualist,
Charlton Beardsley.

Durgan was amazed at such an idea. He remained for some time, as he said to himself,
" convinced " that the mulatto was raving ; and
yet he went as far as to reflect that there had
never been any visible reason for his wife's
devotion to this man ; furthermore, that Bertha
had said that Mr. Claxton, an hour before his
sad death, had received a message from Charlton
Beardsley, that the mulatto had come from
Beardsley, and was it not likely that he had
sought shelter with his employer ? The mulatto
evidently knew Hermione to be innocent ; in
that case Beardsley would know it, and perhaps
Durgan's own wife knew it. They had come
forward with no evidence. What possible motive
could they have had for concealment ?

Durgan broke from his camp bed and from
his hut, hot and stifled by the disagreeable rush
of indignant and puzzled thoughts. He stood
in the free air and dark starlight, trying to shake
off his growing suspicions. Details gathered

from different sources were darting into his mind, and it seemed to him that fancy, not reason, was rapidly constructing a dark story of which he could conceive no explanation, but which involved even himself—through tolerance of his wife's conduct—in the guilt of Miss Claxton's unmerited sufferings.

Alarmed at the trend of these memories and hasty inferences, he controlled himself, to reflect only on the more instant question of Eve's death, and the evidence he must give at the trial. It would appear that until 'Dolphus was condemned, even the Claxtons did not fear his tongue. To give evidence against him, and at the same time to seal his tongue, appeared to be Durgan's immediate duty, but the performance seemed difficult. What bribe, what threat could move a condemned man who was but a waif in the world, and need care for none but himself?

Yet if rational meaning was to be granted at all to his raving on the night of Eve's death, it would appear that even this creature had a reverence for Miss Claxton, and a desire to be the object of her prayers. Was this motive strong enough to be worked upon? It would be better, no doubt, to gain an interview with the prisoner and try to discover if he had any tenacity of purpose, but to this Durgan felt strong repugnance.

In avoiding this issue, his mind began to torment him regarding the evidence against Miss Claxton, which he alone knew, and which he might not have a right to conceal. His ardent belief in her goodness, his firm belief that he had heard Eve die, rested only on intuitive insight, common in men of solitary habit and unscholarly minds; he knew that this was no basis on which to found legal evidence.

With these uneasy and unfinished thoughts he at last fell asleep in the faint light of the dawn, and waked again soon with a vivid and bad dream.

He dreamed that he was again on the lonely mountain on the night of Eve's death, groping under the stunted thicket of old oak. Again he saw Miss Claxton come to the forked tree. She climbed as before, and reached up one thin arm to deposit something in the highest cleft of the trunk. The moon rose as before; Durgan saw in his dream that the thing she hid there was a knife, and the blade was red. Rousing himself from a sleep that brought so odious a vision, he woke to find the rays of a red sunrise in his face.

One of his labourers brought up the borrowed horse which he had arranged to ride to Hilyard. Before he started he went up the trail to the summit house, hoping that Alden might be about. He had nothing definite to ask, and yet he would have been glad to have some parting advice from him. No one was up. The very house was drowsy under the folded petals of its climbing flowers. Durgan went down through the stunted oak wood, and looked up as he passed the forked tree. It was the first time he had been close to it in daylight. In one branch of the fork, close to the notch, there was a round hole, such as squirrels choose for their nests. Better hiding-place for a small object could not be. To act the spy so far as to look into the hole without Miss Claxton's permission would have been what Durgan called "a nigger's trick." Like all the better class of slave-owners, he habitually sought to justify his own assumption of superiority by holding himself high above all mean actions or superstitious ideas. As he went down the hill he was vexed with himself for having been so far influenced by a dream as to have even looked for the hole in the tree.

Yet as he rode out into the glorious morning,

he found himself arguing that if money for the mulatto had been put in the tree, it was odd that the mulatto had made no effort to get it before his arrest or to send for it after. The thing which had really been put there, if not meant for 'Dolphus, was probably intended to be long hidden. But a dream, of course, meant nothing, and his could easily be accounted for by the tenor of his waking thoughts and the colour of the sunrise.

When he reached the saw-mill he turned by the long wooden mill-race and set his horse at a gentle gallop for Hilyard. Even at that speed he began to wonder whether if, by such evidence as had convinced Bertha, he were induced to hold the erroneous opinion of Miss Claxton's guilt, he would be also forced into Bertha's conclusion, that fits of mania were the only explanation. Since last night he had called Bertha a fool; now, while most unwelcome suspicions followed him like tormenting demons, he was driven into greater sympathy with the younger sister.

He galloped gently down the slope of the valley, tree and shrub and flower rushing past him in the freshness of the morning. Suddenly he checked his horse to look up. He was beneath his own precipice. The mine was on a ledge about three hundred feet above him. The rock rose sheer some hundred and fifty feet above that. He could trace the opening of the trail, but even the smoke of the hidden dwelling-house could not be seen here. As Durgan listened for the faint chink of his workmen's tools, and sought from this unfamiliar point of view to trace each well-known spot, he began, for the first time, to realise fully the dreadfulness of the story which only yesterday had revealed.

Involuntarily he drew rein. The memory that had transfixed him was the description of the Claxton murder. While the step-mother had been killed by only one well-aimed shot, the father had been beaten with such brutal rage that no likeness of the living man appeared in the horrid shape of the dead.

He spoke aloud in the sunny solitude, and his words were of Bertha and her sister. " My God ! She has lived alone with her there for two years believing this."

He had very often of late thought slightingly of Bertha's excitability. Last night he had thought scorn of her conclusions. Now, when he perceived how the terrible form of death

N

which had befallen her loved father must have wrought upon her nerves, and how much more reason she had to believe her sister guilty than the most bigoted member of the public who had tried to condemn her, he felt only reverence for the courage and devotion of such a life. No doubt her womanly proneness to nervous fears, and the undisciplined activity of her imagination, had sometimes pictured scenes of impossible distress, and resulted in words and looks inconsistent with her resolution of secrecy; but, also, how much did this timorous and excitable disposition heighten the heroism of the office she had so perseveringly filled.

Yet while he remained in deep admiration of this heroism, he thought that he himself could never forgive Bertha's suspicion of her sister. How much less could Alden forgive? And if it ever reached the trustful mind of that loving sister that the child of her delight had thought her prone to madness, the word "forgiveness" would have no meaning between them. A wound would be made that no earthly love could ever heal.

Bertha's beauty came vividly before him—her kind, honest, impulsive girlhood. "God help her," he said slowly. "She has cheerfully borne worse than hell for love's sake, and such is the extreme tragedy of love, that if she is mistaken, all this loyalty and suffering can never atone for her mistake."

CHAPTER XXIII

DURGAN left the breeze of the sunrise and the mountains behind him, and after that one first gallop, rode slowly down into the stillness of the lower country and the heat of the midday hours. The smoke of some distant forest fire filled the air, diffusing the sunlight in a golden glow. Who can tell the sweetness that the flame of distant pine woods lends? It is not smoke after it has floated many hundred miles; it is a faint and delicious aroma and a tint in the air—that is all.

On the lower side of the road now the hill dropped, in ragged harvest fields and half-cultivated vineyards, towards the wide hot cotton plains of the sea-board. On the other side were enclosed pastures where tame cattle were straying among young growths of trees, which were everywhere again conquering the once smooth clearings.

In the long, central street of Hilyard, behind

the weathered palings, garden flowers brimmed over. Great heads of phlox, white and crimson, sent forth the sweetest and most subtle fragrance. Petunias, large as ladies' bonnets, soft and purple, breathed of honey. Rose and poppy, love-in-a-mist and love-lies-bleeding, marigold and prince's feather, all fought for room in tangles of delight. Over the old wooden houses the morning glory held its gorgeous cups still open under the mellow veil of smoke. No house in the town was newly painted, or bore to the world the sharp, firm outline of good repair; but there was not one which nature had not adorned with flower or vine or moss. Everywhere there was the trace of poverty and languor after war; everywhere there was beauty, sweetness, and warmth, and the gracious outline of repose.

Hilyard lay on the way from the mountains to the broad plantations which still bore Durgan's name. It was soothing to him to find himself again in a country where he had lost so much for the Federal cause that he had gained proportionate respect. The mountain whites knew nothing but their own hills; but here, to everyone, high or low, it was enough that he was Neil Durgan, however shabby his clothes and empty his pocket; and he felt afresh the re-

sponsibility and self-confidence which an honourable ancestry and personal sacrifice have power
to give.

The interview with the magistrate was a short
one. The trial of the two negroes was put off
because the mulatto had asked for ten days in
which to obtain money and advice from his
friends in the North. A few days before Durgan
would have been enraged at the delay on Adam's
account; now he was only too thankful. He
took his resolution, and obtained leave to visit
both prisoners.

The prison was a square house, differing from
others only in having bars in the windows and
standing nakedly to the street without fence or
garden. Outside and in it was dirty and slovenly.
Adam's cell was in bright contrast, well furnished,
clean and neat as its inmate. Adam's skin shone
with soap; his shirt was spotless; he sat on
a rocking-chair, large-print Bible in hand; and
when Durgan came he wept.

"There, there," said Durgan, patting him.
"Reckon you'd better cheer up. The folks all
speak well of you, you big nigger."

The jailer stood in the doorway grinning with
delight at the novel juxtaposition of a good
prisoner and a local hero.

"Oh, Adam," went on Durgan, "you look like a man in a tract. I'm proud of you, Adam. How's this for a good Durgan nigger?" he asked, turning to the hard-featured jailer.

The excellence of Adam's behaviour, which might have been art, had evidently been accepted as artless; for the callous and indolent authorities knew well enough the broad difference between good and bad in the unsophisticated blacks.

"Adam—he does you credit, Mr. Durgan, sir," said the jailer. "Reckon Hilyard always had a good word for your pa's niggers, sir. Adam—he's all right. General Durgan Blount said as how you said he was to have his comforts."

When Durgan stepped again into the dirty passage way, and recalled the turnkey to open the mulatto's cell, all the easy, brutal injustice of it weighed upon his sense of honour; he felt ashamed for his country. 'Dolphus, backed by no local influence, too weak to wash his cell, was confined amid dirt and vermin. The crusted window-glass let in little light. The wretch sat on the edge of a straw bed, almost his only furniture, his silken hair long and matted, his smart clothes crushed, his linen filthy. Durgan was shocked; in such case it was but too evident that his disease, already advanced, would make rapid progress. It was with a new sensation of pity that he took the chair that the jailer thrust in before he withdrew.

"Have you no money to get yourself comforts?" Durgan asked.

"Yes, sir. Miss—that lady, you know, sir—has given me as much as I can spend on food and drink. I ain't got much appetite, sir." He seemed entirely frank as to Miss Claxton's kindness.

"I have come to see if I can do anything for you."

"I thought, sir, you was only the friend of your own niggers like Adam."

"Whom did your father belong to?"

"General Courthope, of Louisiana. No, sir, he isn't dead; but my father ran away when the 'mancipation came, and left the ole Gen'ral, and pulled up in New York; so the fam'ly might as well be dead for all they'll do for me."

"Have you no folks?"

"Not now, sir. I got called for up North, for something I hadn't done; so I had to lie low, and lost any folks I had. But there's one gen'leman I've written to; he'll play up to get me out of this." A curious look came over the face of the speaker. He chuckled.

Durgan felt puzzled at the look and the laugh. "Are you sure he got the letter?"

'Dolphus pulled a well-worn bit of paper out of his pocket. It was a telegram dated only a few days before. He regarded it with an intense expression which might have been hatred, and after gloating over it for a few moments, he showed it to Durgan. It was dated, "Corner of Beard and 84th Street." It said only, "Received letter; you may depend on me." It was signed "B.D." It had been handed in at a New York office two days before.

"And if this friend should fail you?"

"He says, sir, that I can depend upon him; an' I wrote to him that if he didn't come up to the scratch he could depend on me." Another chuckle ended this speech.

"Oh, I see; you have some threat to hold over his head."

'Dolphus did not answer.

Durgan, looking at the lustrous eyes and clever, sickly face, became exceedingly interested in the object of his contemplation. How strange to sit thus face to face, with perhaps nothing between him and the Claxton secret but this dying boy's flimsy will, and yet go away unsatisfied.

Almost in spite of himself, he bent forward and said, "You were in a certain house when a murder was committed. I do not believe you guilty or wish to harm you, but I believe you know who *is* guilty."

A look of caution came over the other's face; he listened and looked intently. "Look here, sir; I wasn't never at no house where there was such things done. I wasn't never at no place such as you say."

Durgan had no argument to meet this obvious lie. He could not quote his authority. He was, however, more interested than angry, because the prisoner was so evidently enjoying the momentous question raised, and with lips parted, sat expectant, as if he did not intend his denial to be believed.

"I only desire to see justice done," said Durgan coldly.

'Dolphus looked at him with eyes half-shut, and, to Durgan's astonishment, a sensation of fear found room in his consciousness. "Are you sure of that, sir?"

"Of what?"

"That you'd like to see justice done—all round, sir?"

"Justice—yes. And what else could I desire

but justice ? " Then he added, hardly knowing why, "But unless you have evidence, no one will believe anything you choose to say."

'Dolphus chuckled aloud. " I've got evidence all right enough, sir ; an' I know where one witness is to be found—a truthful lady, sir, who is so queer made that she'd die rather than hurt a gen'leman she cared for, sir ; but she'd sooner hurt him than swear what was false. I'm agoin' to clear her in spite of herself."

" Do you wish to hurt this good lady by making her real name known here where she wishes it to be concealed ? "

" Look you here, sir. You're a mighty fine gen'leman ; I'm a poor yaller nigger ; you wouldn't trust me with a ten-cent bit. Well, sir ; one of us has got to give a good deal to save that lady. Which 'ull it be, sir ? "

Durgan received this astonishing challenge in amazement. He began to believe the fellow was in terrible earnest under his mocking tone and light manner. He was too proud to answer.

" Look here, sir ; you can go an' tell that pious little lady I won't harm her—not if I die for it ; but I ain't goin' to die till I've done better than that. I'm turning ill now, sir. You'd

better send for the man outside to bring me
something to drink. I'll pay him, sir."

He actually refused the greenbacks his visitor
offered. Before Durgan had summoned the
turnkey, 'Dolphus had curled himself up on the
pallet in all the appearance of a swoon.

Durgan went to the "hotel" where he had
left his horse. It was a wooden house with
scanty furniture, all its many doors and windows
open to the street. Two old women sat in one
doorway, ceaselessly rubbing their gums with
snuff—a local vice. Three rickety children were
playing in the bar-room. The landlord was ex-
ercising his thoroughbred horses in the yard.
The horses were beautiful creatures, neither
rickety nor vicious.

A valuable microscope and a case of surgical
instruments stood on a table, surrounded by the
ash of cigars. They were the property of the
country doctor, a noted surgeon, who was satisfied to make his home in this fantastic inn. The
wife of the hotel-keeper, who always wore a blue
sun-bonnet whether in or out of the house,
brought Durgan a glass of the worst beer he had
ever tasted, and delicious gingerbread hot from
the oven.

When Durgan had found the doctor and made

sure that he would go at once and better the mulatto's condition, he set out on his homeward journey. He had said to the medical man, "Whatever happens, you must not let the fellow die till I come back."

The answer had been, "I won't do that."

CHAPTER XXIV

DURGAN had ridden down the hills in rather
leisurely fashion ; now he urged his horse
to speed. He had come uncertain how to meet
the issue of the day ; now he was eager to fore-
stall the issue of the next.

He had brought from his interview with the
dying prisoner a strong impression that the poor
fellow had more mind and purpose than he had
supposed, and that he certainly had some scheme
on hand from the development of which he expected excitement and some lively satisfaction.

The hints thrown out sounded madder than
the supposed raving of his last night of freedom.
He had control over some unknown person, or
persons, of wealth in New York, who would
send to save him, and he would sacrifice something—perhaps his salvation—to Miss Claxton ;
further, he threatened Durgan with discomfiture.

What could seem more mad than all this ?
But to-day Durgan was not at all sure that the

poor creature did not mean all he said and could not do all he promised. The development of the mulatto's purpose might be left to time, but Durgan's purpose was to follow up the clues he had obtained, and two facts had to be dealt with now. 'Dolphus had freely expressed the belief that Miss Claxton had shielded an unknown criminal of the male sex whom she loved. Durgan had been so astonished, and even shocked, at hearing his own bold surmise so quickly and fully corroborated, that he knew now for the first time how little confidence he had had in his own detective powers. Further, it was probably this guilty person over whom 'Dolphus had power. He was rich, and could not be unknown; he was within reach, for he had recently telegraphed, and the address given must be meant to find him. Durgan felt that it would be criminal to lose a moment in putting this clue in Alden's hand.

Bertha had desired that Alden should be left in ignorance of the mulatto's identity because she feared it might lead to her sister's condemnation; now that 'Dolphus himself had implied that he could clear the sister's reputation, Bertha could not, must not, hesitate. Miss Claxton's desire to hide from Alden who the mulatto was and what he knew must be part of her desire to hide the miscreant : but with time, Durgan was ready to believe, this desire must have lessened or almost failed, as love must have cooled. In any case, Miss Claxton held all her desires as subordinate to the will of God ; persuasion, reason, pressure, must move her. Durgan urged on his horse.

All the way home he passed over shady roads flecked with pink sunlight. The heaviest foliage of summer mantled the valleys. The birds were almost still, resting in the deep shadows of the mature season.

When Durgan was almost within hearing of the waterfall and the hum of the saw-mill at Deer Cove, he met three riders. Mr. Alden and Bertha, in company with young Blount, were descending for a gallop in the cool of the evening. They all stopped to say they had heard by post that the trial was deferred, and to inquire after Adam's welfare.

Durgan could reply cheerfully as to Adam, that he was spending his time in ablutions and pious exercises, and that the authorities were bent upon having him acquitted.

"Reckon they are," said young Blount. "My father saw to that when he went over."

Durgan saw that neither Bertha nor Mr. Alden would ask about the other prisoner in his cousin's presence. He said in a casual tone, "The yellow fellow seems assured that he will have money and influence behind him, too, by next week."

"Yes," cried Blount, interested always in minutiæ, "he sent a letter and received a telegram."

Durgan rode on. He must wait now an hour or two for an opportunity to speak to Alden or Bertha, and he began to wonder whether it would not be more honourable to approach Miss Claxton direct, confess what he had chanced to see of her secret actions, and tell her frankly what the mulatto had let fall that day. His borrowed horse had been offered the hospitality of her stable for the night, so he must, perforce, reach the summit.

The horse rubbed down and fed in the spacious stable, Durgan sought the front of the low house, now richly decorated by the scarlet trumpet-flower, which had conquered the other creepers of earlier summer, and had thrown out its triumphal flag from the very chimneys.

He found the lady, as he had expected, sitting quietly busy at some woman's work in the front porch. The house mastiff lay at her feet, and

o

round the corner came the low, sweet song of the coloured maid who had taken Eve's place in the kitchen. The rich crimson plant called "love-lies-bleeding," now in full flower, trailed its tassels on the earth on either side of the low doorway. It seemed, indeed, a fit emblem of the tragedy of the life beside it.

Miss Claxton welcomed Durgan with her usual self-effacing gentleness. "Bertha and Mr. Alden have ridden out with Mr. Blount. Thought likely you would have met them."

Durgan's avowal of the meeting caused her to expect an explanation of his visit; but for some minutes he dallied, glad to rest in her gentle presence, and feeling now the extreme difficulty of saying things he thought it only honourable to say.

He had hitherto blamed Bertha and Alden for not addressing themselves to Miss Claxton more openly. He now realised to what degree she had the power which many of the meekest people possess, of hiding from the strife of tongues behind their own gentle, inapproachable dignity.

Durgan rested in pacific mood while she uttered gentle words of sympathy for his fatigue, and fell into a muse of astonishment that she should be the centre of such pressing and tragic interests. So strong was his silent thought that it would have forced him into questions had she been less strong. He longed to ask, " Why do you assume that this 'Dolphus will not expose the criminal you have suffered so much to hide ? "

Instead, he only began to describe his visits to the prisoners, taking Adam first, and coming naturally to 'Dolphus.

" It was real kind of you, Mr. Durgan, to see after him ; and it was very mean of the jail folks not to wash up for him. He had money to pay them."

"The doctor will make them stand round. But I wanted to tell you that I have been wondering upon what or whom 'Dolphus relies for his defence. Adam has such a strong backing, there seems to be no doubt of his acquittal. I did not know this till I went to-day, or how little difference the emancipation has really made as to the justice or injustice meted out to niggers. I supposed—I have been absent since the close of the war—that the evidence given at the trial would be all-important. Now I think the conclusion is foregone ; judge and jury, whoever the jurors may be, have already fallen into the belief that I and my cousins have insisted on."

She had dropped her work ; she was absorbed
in his every word. "It's a bad principle, of
course," she said ; "but as to Adam, it is working out all right. I suppose—I suppose, Mr.
Durgan, that 'Dolphus did kill poor Eve ? I'd
feel pretty mean if he's being punished for
nothing."

"I believe he did ; but I have no proof."

"I don't mind telling you, Mr. Durgan, that
I got Mr. Alden to get a lawyer—quite privately,
of course—to offer his services to 'Dolphus—to
tell him we would pay the costs, because Adam
and Eve were our 'help,' and of course we
wanted to see only justice done. 'Dolphus
wouldn't accept it. He refused ; we don't know
why. He told the lawyer he knew 'a game
worth two of that.' Of course, if there is mis-
carriage of justice, we can't feel quite so badly as
if we hadn't made the offer."

"What do you think he meant by 'knowing a
better game'?"

"It wasn't just fooling, was it, Mr. Durgan?"
Underneath her quiet there was now a tremulous
eagerness ; her faded eyes looked to his with
sorrowful appeal.

"No ; after seeing him to-day, I am inclined
to think more of him than I did ; but I think

he's up to tricks of some sort.   May I tell you what he said to me, Miss Claxton ?"

" I'm just praying to the Lord all the time, Mr. Durgan, and trying to leave it all in His hands.   He won't let us suffer more than is right ; and I hope He'll give us grace to bear what He sends, if it isn't the full deliverance I pray for."

Durgan was nonplussed.   " Do you mean to say you would rather not hear what the man said ? because I must tell Alden, and as it concerns you most, I thought——"

" Yes, I guess perhaps I ought to hear it. And if you tell me you don't need to tell Mr. Alden, because I know better than you what he ought to hear—that is, if it concerns me."

This seemed a simple and self-evident view of the case ; Durgan hardly knew how he could have thought of interfering.   Nor did he find it at all easy to put significance into the prisoner's words apart from his own foreknowledge and prejudgment of the case.

" 'Dolphus suggested to me that I would not wish to see justice done in—to say the truth—in your own case, Miss Claxton.   He challenged me, asking if I were willing to make a sacrifice to prove your innocence."

She looked at him straight. Her eyes were not faded now; he was amazed at the flash and flush of energy and youth he had brought to her face. He thought he had never in his life seen so honest, so spiritual a face as that which confronted him; but whether her present expression was one of astonishment or dismay he could not tell.

"You could not have expected him to speak on this subject; and you never had any connection with our trouble? What more did he say?"

"He never really mentioned your name; I only assumed that his reference was to you. He said that he knew a lady who would die to save a—well, he *said*, a gentleman she loved, but would let even *him* die rather than swear falsely."

She never flinched. "Was that all?" she asked.

But Durgan was already cut with remorse to think how impertinent his words must sound. "No, that was not all. He asked me to give you a message, to tell you that he would not harm you—that he would rather die than harm you. This was in answer to my suggestion that you would not wish your real name to be known in these parts."

She looked relieved. "I have always believed

that he had more good in him than you thought. But tell me all. I'd liefer hear every word, if you please."

"I hope I remember all that he said. I think that was all that I took to be a direct reference to you, Miss Claxton ; but what I thought most needful to tell Alden——"

"Yes ?" The little word pulsed with restrained excitement.

"I asked the fellow on what defence he relied, and he said what made me think he had the pull of some threat over the person he relied on. He had had a telegram."

"I don't exactly understand, Mr. Durgan."

"Neither do I, I assure you."

"But I mean, what has that to do with Mr. Alden ?"

"Oh, I think I assumed that 'Dolphus believed this person to be the criminal, and his address was on the telegram."

"May I ask why you made this assumption ?"

"It may have been unwarranted, but taken in connection with his boast that he could establish your entire freedom from blame——" Durgan was floundering in his effort to find words for the very painful subject. He paused, with face red and dew on his brow.

"I guess, Mr. Durgan, if you'll speak quite plainly what you mean, it will be better for us both."

"Why do you include me? Do you know why this boy threatens me, reproaches me, challenges me?"

"Tell me first, Mr. Durgan, what you made out, and what you think this telegram has to do with it?"

"To be plain, I suspect that this man knows who was guilty of the crime for which you were tried, that he is now in communication with him, and I saw an address in the telegram he had received."

"What was the address?"

"'Corner of Beard and 84th Street,' and it was signed 'B.D.'" He told her its contents.

She went into the house and brought out a New York directory a year or two old. "I guess there isn't any such corner," she said, and in a moment she showed him there was not.

"Do you know of anyone who has these initials?"

"I do not."

"If Alden sent a detective to the office where it was received, I wonder if he could find out who sent it."

" Is it likely that if anyone took the trouble to give a wrong address, they would leave any clue to their whereabouts ? "

" Could 'Dolphus give Alden any information of moment ? "

" He could give him none that would do anyone any good."

" Might that not be a matter of opinion ? "

" I don't see that folks who don't know what they are doing can have a right to an opinion about the results."

There was then a silence. The sun had long set on the valley, but from this eminence its last rays were still seen mingling with a foam of crimson cloud in a vista of the western hills. Both the man and woman had their faces turned to the great red cloud-flower in which the light of day was declining. The mountains were solemn and tender ; the valleys dim and wide. It was not a scene on which the sober mind could gaze without gaining for the hour some reflection of the greatness and earnestness of God.

But the world about could only be an environment to their thought, not for a moment its object. Durgan was roused in spirit. The quiescent temper which he had sought to obtain in compensation for a stormy and disappointed youth was lost for the time. This woman, who bore the odium of a cruel and dastardly deed, was still intent on shielding the real doer. Durgan looked at the splendid arena of the mountains and the manifest struggle of light and darkness therein; the many tracks of suspicion in which his thoughts had all day been moving gathered together.

"Miss Claxton, are you willing to tell me all you know about Charlton Beardsley?"

She looked at him for a moment as if trying to read his thoughts, then looked back at the outer world, as if moved by his question only to profound and regretful reverie.

"About Charlton Beardsley I know very little," she said, in a voice touched as with compassion; "very, very little, Mr. Durgan; but I had once occasion to ask your wife something about him, and she told me, I believe truly, that he had been brought up, an orphan, in an English charity school, that he had no relatives that he knew of and no near friends. That was all she could tell me. He was by taste a somewhat solitary mystic, I believe, only sought after by those who had discovered his delusions and wished to be deluded by them. You see, I can easily tell you all I know; it is not much."

Durgan sat watching her, too entirely amazed at both words and manner to find speech. Just so a good woman, treading the violets of some neglected graveyard, might speak of the innocent dead who lay beneath.

There was silence.

Miss Claxton said, "I always like the time just after the sun goes down, Mr. Durgan; I have a fancy it is the time one feels nearest God. I suppose it's only fancy, but it does say in Genesis, you know, that God walked in the garden in the cool of the day."

Then, as darkness grew, and finding that he made no response, she exerted herself and rose to light the lamp.

In the full light she faced him. "Mr. Durgan, I don't wonder you feel the responsibility of the suspicions the negro has put into your mind. I don't blame you, and it's only natural he should like the excitement of talking. It would not be right for me to tell you exactly what I believe he was referring to; but there are some things I can tell you, and I can only pray God to help you to believe what I say. I believe it was your wife who sent that telegram; it was, at least, paid for with her money, and it will be her money that will be used freely to get 'Dolphus acquitted. If you pursue the suspicions he has started for you, I don't believe you will make any discovery. But even if you did, what would happen? You would drag your wife's name in the mire; you would"—she paused, and tried to steady her voice. "Oh, Mr. Durgan, think of Bertha; you would break Bertha's heart and mine. You think you understand justice, and that there is someone whom you ought to bring to justice. Justice belongs to God. He alone can mete it out in this world so as to save the soul that has sinned. Are you afraid to leave it to Him? I am not. I have left it to Him for five years, and I am not sorry, but glad. And I entreat you to consider that if you interfere you don't know what you are doing; you may make the worst mistakes. 'Dolphus thinks he knows the name of the person who should be brought to justice; I assure you he does not. I spoke to him on the night Eve died, and found out that he did not. Believe me, Mr. Durgan, I am making no romantic and fantastic sacrifice of myself, as this negro supposes. The truth, were it made public, would be the worst thing for me, as for Bertha, and would bring yourself shame and pain. And it could never be the real, whole truth, for that you could not understand, nor could anyone. I hear their horses on the hill. Please go. Do not let them find you here, as if you had had news of some strange thing. You know nothing, for the thing you think you know is not true. Do nothing, for fear you do harm. You cannot do any good."

"But how can you be sure this sick man will not do the thing you dread?"

"I begged him not to do anything, just as I've begged you. I don't think, anyway, that he will get the chance he reckons on. If he did, I think that when he has to choose between accepting the help that will get him acquitted, if anything will, of the present charge against him, and, as he thinks, righting me, the love of life will be too strong. He will not die on my behalf, even though his intentions are good, as I believe yours are, Mr. Durgan."

Durgan had turned to the door the moment she had asked him to go. He was tarrying on the threshold to ask his last question, to hear her response. When he heard himself, with no unkind intent, naturally linked with the wretched mulatto, his pace was accelerated. With a word of farewell he disappeared into the dusk, hearing the horses arrive at the stables as he went his fugitive way down the familiar trail.

CHAPTER XXV

DURGAN had still one strong emotion regarding his wife: he was able to feel overwhelming shame on her account, and he dreaded any publicity concerning her behaviour. She had always lived so as to command the consent of good society to her doings. He had perfectly trusted her social instinct to do this as long as it lay in her power to tell her own story; but he knew, with a sense of bitter degradation, that if someone else had need to tell that story, it would sound very different.

His wife was the daughter of an uneducated hotel-keeper, and had married him, as he afterwards discovered, because he had the entrance into certain drawing-rooms and clubs, which, if skilfully used, might have proved the stepping-stone to almost any social eminence. At the time of her marriage she had professed passionate love for him and sympathy for the Southern cause; and her fortune, not small, was naturally

to be used in the difficult task of making part of
his paternal acres productive by the paid labour
of the negroes reared and trained by his father
and justly dear to the son.   Disconsolate at the
loss of friends and fortune—for all near to him
had died in the war, of wounds or sorrow—
Durgan repaid the love and sympathy of one who
seemed a warm-hearted and impulsive woman
with tender gratitude.

A little later, when the wife found out that
Durgan would not push himself into the fashionable *milieu* which was open to him in Europe and
America, he began to discover, though slowly,
that she would not bestow affection or time on
any less fashionable pursuit.   She needed her
whole fortune for the social adventures that she
must make alone ; and as he would not open the
door of Southern pride for her, she fell to knock-
ing at the door of Northern pride for herself.
No doubt Providence has a good reason for
making men before marriage blind to female
character, but it was many years before Durgan
bowed to the fate to which defect, not fault, had
brought him.   Too proud to accept any bounty
from such a wife, he had sullenly shielded her
from remark till she reached a position of middle-
class fashion in which she could stand alone.

Having attempted, in the meantime, to increase by speculation the small patrimony left him, and losing much, he had retired from the scene of her struggles some six years before the present time, proudly thankful that any public reproach was directed only at himself. Since then she had scaled social heights seemingly beyond her —he had often wondered how.

That this wife was tricky and false, that the means she had used to cajole or overawe the society she was determined to conquer bore no necessary relation to the truth, he knew; but knowing her also to be clever and cold-hearted, he had not feared that she would so transgress any social law as to make her small or large meannesses known.

But the most surprising thing in his wife's career since he left her was that she had not dropped the medium, Beardsley, as soon as his health and popularity were lost. She had been wont to drop all her instruments as soon as their use was over, and most of them had more attractions than he. The man had been poor, plebeian, and sickly; and Durgan, who had never suspected love as the cause of the odd relationship, had now some cause to suppose it rooted in the unspeakable shame of the worst

P

of crimes. In what possible way this had come
about he could not even begin to imagine, but
he continued to consider his maturing suspicion
in growing consternation.

If Miss Claxton had not told him the truth,
she was a more finished actress than the world
had yet seen. If what she said of his wife were
true, the mulatto's words were corroborated—
his wife was nearly connected with this awful
crime.

In Durgan's mind the telegraphic address—
evidently suggestive to Miss Claxton—had at
last become significant. "Beard" suggested
Beardsley; "84" was the date of the Claxton
murder; "B" might possibly stand for Beardsley, and "D" for his wife. Then the help
promised evidently involved his wife's purse.
Beardsley had nothing.

If this Beardsley was guilty, he must be a
most extraordinary man. It was clear that if it
was he whom Hermione Claxton was shielding,
she was as much determined to keep his secret
to-day as at first. She could not speak of him
save in tones of sorrow and tenderness. For
him, too, the wife whom Durgan knew to be
cold and ambitious had apparently ventured all.
The extraordinary nature of a man who could

on short acquaintance so deeply involve two such different women, gave Durgan so much room for astonished thought that some other things Miss Claxton had said for the time escaped his memory.

His strongest impulse after the last interview was to take Miss Claxton at her word and make no further move in the matter—at least, not now and on her account. Ultimately he must find out if his wife was in any plot to conceal a criminal, and if so, put a stop to her connivance. At present he had certainly no desire to make such action on his wife's part public, or break Bertha's heart by filling the air with a public scandal in which her sister's name would be linked with a lover who was a common charlatan and brutal criminal. If for this man's sake Hermione had left her father's death unavenged and ruined her sister's life, Bertha's wrath and sorrow might well be a thing to dread, and such knowledge a disaster that might well crush her. The mulatto might work to bring truth to light; he must work alone.

But at this point Durgan again shifted his ground of suspicion; for he still believed in Hermione Claxton's singular purity of mind and gentleness of disposition, and in his wife's callousness and shrewd selfishness. Was it possible that Beardsley had some mysterious power over both women such as a magician or modern hypnotist is said to use? But then, was not such influence in such a man too strange to be possible, too like a cheap novel to be true? A terrible thought struck cold at Durgan's heart; the man, as he knew of him, was more likely to be a cat's-paw than the mover in any momentous deed. The surprise of ascertaining that his wife had had some connection with the Claxtons forced him to realise how little he knew about her life, how totally ignorant he was as to any cause she might have to hate Mr. and Mrs. Claxton. His heart failed him.

He drew in his breath in quick terror, trying to persuade himself that he could not have arrived at the bottom of a secret over which Alden had brooded so long in vain.

"Well, I understand that your visit to Hilyard was most satisfactory. You are assured of your good Adam's safety; and I find the mulatto sent a message to our friends that he would not drag their name into the business. So far so good. Do you suppose that the money and advice he expects to receive are all in the air, or how?" Alden, dandified and chirpy, his little grey beard wagging in the morning sunlight, was standing on the mountain road. There was a sharpness as of autumn in the sunshine, which made the New Yorker fresh. Durgan, who had taken to his pick and spade very early that morning, already warm, dirty, and tired, looked like some grim demiurge. Called from his work to this colloquy, he was not in good humour.

"These fellows are always boasting," continued Alden. "The peculiarity in this case is that he would not take the cost of his own defence from us."

"And *I* offered him what I had in my pocket. He would not look at it," said Durgan dully.

"Odd."

"Do you think so ?"

"Well, of course, when a flimsy, tawdry creature of that sort refuses a bird in the hand, one wonders what he sees in the bush, especially when, as in this case, the bird in hand could hardly prevent his robbing the bush also."

"I reckon it's beyond me," said Durgan stupidly. Alden's simile reminded him afresh of the hole in the forked tree, which had not ceased to haunt his mind.

"You have a headache this morning, my dear sir."

"Thanks; I'm all right."

A boy, a slovenly country lout, came up the hill. He was whistling a merry air attuned to the snap of the morning. He was looking about him in the trees for birds and squirrels. His hands hung in the delicious idleness of his pockets. There was a spring in his legs to match his tone. Durgan envied him unfeignedly. He thought of his own gallant, cheerful purpose of the day before, and wished that he dare form any fresh resolve. Alden was evidently alarmed by what he had heard.

"As you know, being widely known as counsel for the Claxtons, I preferred not to appear to take any interest in this prisoner. A possible inference might have been drawn by someone. We of the law, my dear sir——"

Durgan perceived that it would be a vast relief to his conscience if Alden could visit 'Dolphus himself.

"They are lax," continued Alden; "there would be no difficulty in my seeing the man."

"Why do you want to see him?"

"I hear he wrote to New York and got a telegram back. He may, for all we know, be a member of a gang of thieves or blackmailers. They may bribe judge and jury with a thousand

dollars if he threatens to round on them. A
little money would go a long way in Hilyard.
Then, if it is proved, so to say, that both
prisoners are innocent, the authorities might
arrest someone else."

"Me, for instance? I was there."

"Probably not you!" Then after a pause he
added, "Miss Claxton is disposed to think that
we have done all we can honestly do, and must
now leave the matter in the hand of Providence;
but, under Providence, I myself feel that I am
responsible for leaving no effort untried to
gain further light as to the basis of this fellow's
hopes."

The boy, bobbing his head, explained to Durgan
that he had been sent to fetch the borrowed horse.

When he had gone on, Durgan said, "'Dolphus
may die before anything happens; that would be
the simplest solution, perhaps." He remembered
how yesterday it had seemed all-important to
extract all the knowledge this man had before
life went from him.

"Ah; you spoke to the doctor, I hear. It is
always right, in any case, to preserve life as long
as possible."

Durgan looked toward his mine. The triteness
to which the dialogue had descended was the more

irksome because he suspected that Alden read beneath his own sudden dullness and inertia.

"When the boy brings along the horse you can ride it as far as my cousins'. He will find you a buggy, and will give you a letter which will open things at Hilyard without giving much publicity to your own name and position. But you, of course, can best judge whether it's worth while to go."

"Miss Claxton has seemed averse to my going," said Alden ; and because Durgan made no answer to this, he sat down on a rock, with brows knit, and determined to go.

Some twenty minutes later Durgan was called again into the road. The lout of a boy refused to give Alden the horse. He said very little ; he even blubbered ; but he hung on to the bridle and tried to pass.

It was soon discovered that he had been commissioned by Miss Claxton to take a telegram to Hilyard, for which service he had been promised excessive pay.

Wrath rose in Durgan. "Fool that I was to warn her," he thought. "She has wired to the man she shields to be on his guard." At that moment his wife's welfare was not in his thought, and he felt he would rather have suffered the last penalty of crime himself than allow this coil of secrets to exist longer. He inwardly cursed all women, and was very sorry for Alden.

Alden, meanwhile, unconscious of need for passion, was explaining that he knew what the telegram must be, as he had heard Miss Claxton mention that some supplies on which she was depending were delayed. As he was going he would assume the responsibility of sending it. He would pay the boy.

Durgan was afraid to speak. He picked up the boy, took a letter addressed to the telegraph clerk out of his pocket, and sent him running down the road at a forced pace. He put the sealed message in Alden's hand, and returned to his work before a word could escape his lips.

As he toiled all day with spade and mattock, he wondered incessantly whether or not Alden would open the message to see it correctly transmitted.

When the long work day had calmed his pulse he was still too impatient to wait Alden's time; sauntered down the hill, and finally reached Deer Cove.

There he saw Alden looking very tired and haggard, but in no haste to return.

The saw-mill was silent for the night. The

quiet plash of the water over the dam made a pleasing accompaniment to a banjo played by a negro. The musician sat on the steps of the general store and post-office; he wore a red handkerchief on his head. Some of his kind were dancing in leisurely burlesque in an open space between the steps and the mill-race. A circle of white men looked on, exchanging foolish jokes and puffing strong tobacco. Many a bright necktie or broad-brimmed hat gave picturesqueness to the group. The quiet of the sylvan evening was over and around them all.

Alden, standing on the verandah of the post-office, looking upon this scene as if he were an habitual lounger, struck Durgan as presenting one of the saddest figures he had ever seen. No sign that could be controlled of any grief was there; but the incongruity between what the man was doing, and what in a better state of mind he would have liked to do, seemed to betoken a depression so deep that normal action was inhibited for the time.

Durgan thought one of the Blounts was perhaps with Alden. He accordingly went straight inside the store; but the place was empty. No one of gentle birth was to be seen near or far. When he came out on the verandah Alden explained that he had insisted on leaving the trap at the Blounts' and walking. " I was stiff with the drive and felt the walk would do me good. You found me resting by the way."

Durgan remarked that there was nothing like a leisurely walk when cramped with sitting long.

After a while the two were beginning the ascent of Deer together, still uttering trivial words.

CHAPTER XXVI

" DID you see the prisoners ? " asked Durgan. He assumed that Alden would visit Adam as a blind.

" Ah—I saw the doctor. It occurred to me to see him first."

" How long will 'Dolphus live ? " asked Durgan eagerly. Again he felt that he could not let this man die without extracting whatever clue he held.

" Impossible to make any forecast. The doctor has had the glass removed from his window—in short, the proper steps are being taken. Absolute quiet is ordered."

" Then you *could* not see him ? "

" No."

After a minute Alden sat down wearily on a fallen tree. The wood was close upon them on all sides. The crescent moon, like a golden boat sailing westward, was seen through chinks in the leafy roof.

"I sent him a message to say that if there was anything he wished done, he might trust me to do it. I made sure that the doctor, honest man, would impress on him the fact that I, too, am honest."

"That doctor *is* a man to be relied on. It's wonderful how one comes across an honest man once in a while."

"Mr. Durgan, when I first related to you my clients' unfortunate story, you were kind enough to express your faith and reverence for such a woman as Miss Claxton, and your willingness to serve her. I felt very grateful to you. I should like to speak to you in confidence, and take counsel with you now."

Durgan sat still, suspecting that he might be subjected to the subtle cross-questioning for which Alden was celebrated.

Alden continued : "I naturally asked the clerk to read Miss Claxton's telegrams to see if he understood them. There are so often errors of transcription."

"There were two, then ?"

"One was, as I had supposed, about the supplies. I did not send the other. It is about that I wish to consult you. The address of Mrs. Durgan is——? "

Durgan gave a number on Fifth Avenue.

"I supposed as much. The message was addressed quite openly to Charlton Beardsley at that address. It said, 'Lost article being traced. Reward likely to be claimed.' It was not signed. Why is this man kept under your wife's roof?"

"As a sort of adviser in occult matters— as one might say, a spiritual director."

"There is only one reward with which the Claxtons have any interest. That is offered for information concerning the murderer."

"I thought it was offered for the missing boy."

"It's all the same. Whoever can be proved to have been in the house at the time, having hidden himself afterwards, must have been in some way concerned with the murder. The laws of chance preclude the idea of there being two mysteries in one house at one time. I now ask you, would you have advised me to send this telegram without further information? It goes to a house over which you have at least some legal control."

Durgan perceived that it was any information he might possess, rather than advice, that Alden really sought; but determined only to give advice. His thoughts and passions had been wavering this way and that for twenty-four hours; now he knew his mind, and answered Alden's question. "It lies in a nutshell," said he. "Are you able to trust Miss Claxton's goodness against all evidence to the contrary, or are you not? You have assured me that no one who knew her could mistrust her; and you, of all people, not only know her best, but, pardon me, love her. If you trust her you should have sent the telegram and asked no questions. If not, set your detectives to work, for I don't believe you will learn anything further from Miss Claxton."

Alden turned on him fiercely. "You know more than you say in this matter. You are trying to shield your wife."

"As far as I know, my wife has done nothing wrong. As to Miss Claxton, I have known her only a few months, and that slightly. I see clearly, as you do, that facts point to some underhand dealing on her part. Further, I have been taught from my childhood to distrust anyone who uses hackneyed religious phrases as she does. In spite of all this I believe in her. I cannot conceive of any circumstance that could justify her secrecy and double-dealing; but I believe there is a justification. Is not that about what you feel too?"

"You speak somewhat evasively, Mr. Durgan. You can surely tell me more about your wife than about Miss Claxton. It was not until I read this message that I knew—what I never could have supposed—that any member of your household could be guilty of any connection with that crime. You must see that it now becomes my positive duty to make the strictest inquiry."

"Why—if Miss Claxton does not wish it? If she was, through your exertions, acquitted, she has, as you know, suffered the penalty of the crime ten times over. If she prefers to continue that pain and ignominy rather than allow you to again open the inquiry, what right have you, as her friend and agent, to reopen it?"

"I owe a higher allegiance—to the law of my country, and the law of my God."

"And when these laws conflict, I presume you would wish to obey the latter? My notion is that Miss Claxton's conduct indicates such a conflict." Durgan's voice was still hard and cold.

"I should need to be assured of such contradiction."

"Are you not willing to give her the benefit of the presumption?"

There is not a man on earth who is content to be alone. Durgan, recently horror-stricken at the thought of the part his wife might have played, realised how little reason he had to feel such blind confidence in anyone whom he had the right to love, and envied Alden his opportunity for faith. Nothing like starvation to give a man a clear sight of another's luxuries and corresponding duties.

"In the war," he added, "we Southerns had to learn to trust out and out whom we trusted at all."

"That Miss Claxton is doing what she conceives to be right, I have no doubt," said Alden stiffly.

Even in the dim light there was a visible improvement of attitude; some heart for life appeared to return to him with this declaration, which a moment before would have been a lie. Durgan could almost have laughed out in irony.

"What she supposes to be right," repeated the reviving lover ; "but I cannot approve."

"She is a reasonable woman; you ought to trust her reason. As you don't know what she is doing, you don't know whether you approve or not."

"*You* know what she is doing, Mr. Durgan. You have information from Mrs. Durgan or Beardsley that I have not."

Q

"No; if my wife is in it, I have been as completely hoodwinked as you. I cannot even yet imagine how my wife could be inculpated in any way. And this Beardsley—I know nothing more of him than I told you; and the only explanation I can suggest as to the message you hold is merely the crudest imagination : supposing him to be the guilty person, Miss Claxton must have been in love with him to shield him as she did—as she does. You cannot wish that made public."

Alden rose up, his back stiff with indignation. "Sir ! that is at least a contingency which is entirely impossible. Are you aware that, before her father's death, Hermione Claxton had consented to marry me ? We were about to make the engagement public. I had asked Mr. Claxton to accord me an interview. He was a confirmed hypochondriac; it was difficult to see him. I was waiting his pleasure when the tragedy—— Ah ! it is impossible to explain how this tragedy has wrecked our lives, for, with an unparalleled strength of will and sensitive honour, Miss Claxton at once, and ever since, has refused to link her name with mine. But one thing, at least, this relation gives me reason to assure you : before this crime Miss Claxton had not a serious thought that she did not confide to me. There was no one on earth that she would wish to shield in the way you suggest; I know there was not. Her father, and her anxiety concerning the state of irreligion in which he lived; her sister, whom she loved with a mother's love; her mission work, which with her was done as under a direct command from our Lord—these, and the friendship she felt for my unworthy self, made up her life. I am certain of that, sir. As for this Beardsley, she not only despised him as a common impostor, but she abhorred him for the hold he had over her father."

"Your view, then, coincides with that of her sister," Durgan pondered, as he spoke.

The lawyer's eyelids flickered at this use of Bertha's name.

"So," continued Durgan, "to come to the point; what do you suppose this intercepted message means?"

"The mulatto, you tell me, expected a large sum of money to be expended on his defence. Our first supposition to account for this was that he might be one of a gang and his fellows would buy him off. I judge now, rather, that he must have information that would enable him to claim the reward in the Claxton case. It must have

228 THE EARTHLY PURGATORY

been the possession of this information that brought him round this neighbourhood. This telegram seems to show that what you told Miss Claxton yesterday led her to believe he was about to claim it. As I read it, she wishes, through Beardsley, to warn someone on whom she believes the suspicion likely to fall."

"But you say there can be no one whom Miss Claxton would wish to shield."

The lawyer's whole manner faltered. "I could not have believed it," he said. "I may say I cannot believe it now."

"My suspicions centre on Beardsley himself," Durgan said, "and I cannot understand why, at the time of the trial, the clue afforded by the note brought by the missing boy was not closely followed up. Beardsley, I happen to know, was seriously ill shortly after the crime, for he was at my wife's house; but, as he sent the boy, he must have been able to give some suggestion as to where he came from or went to. I cannot understand when you sought for the boy why he was not cross-questioned."

Alden got up, and they began to ascend the road.

"I am interested in the result of any mature reflection of yours, Mr. Durgan. I notice that your observations are astute." He walked, his head slightly bent, in an attitude of attention.

"I can't understand," said Durgan, "why it was assumed at the trial that this note was merely a begging letter. My belief is that it gave a warning of someone's visit."

Alden put in : "It is true Miss Claxton said at the inquest that she had not seen its contents."

Durgan spoke with increasing eagerness. "But she said at the same time that she knew it came from Charlton Beardsley. Her very words were, 'From that impostor Beardsley.'"

"Your memory is evidently good. And this might have suggested to you, at any rate, that she could have no affection for Beardsley. But I have been thinking that perhaps you are right ; the clue of the note was not followed up as it ought to have been."

"You must have seen Beardsley. How did he convince you that he could throw no light on the whereabouts of the missing boy ? What did he say was in the note ? " Durgan turned upon his companion almost angrily, and saw the little grey-haired man walking steadily on with abstracted mien. But there was a peculiar aspect of attention about his shoulders, his neck ; it seemed to alter the very shape of his ears.

Durgan felt himself warned of some unseen pitfall. "You must consider my crude way of dealing with a problem to which you have brought your highly trained mind somewhat absurd," he said.

"By no means. I am only surprised at your able handling of the matter, and—ah—a little surprised, perhaps, at some omissions which seem to have occurred in my conduct of the case. May I ask you, Mr. Durgan, if you have had any corroboration of the idea that this note came from Beardsley, either from him or from your wife?"

"No. Certainly not. I only know what Miss Claxton said before the coroner."

"Miss Claxton never gave that evidence. Until you told me a moment ago I never heard the note came from Beardsley. I am shocked and surprised."

Durgan started. "Surely I am quoting the verbatim report."

"I can see, Mr. Durgan, that you believe Miss Claxton did say this; and as it was not given publicly, someone must have told you in private. I will not ask you again the source of your information, which I now suppose to have been Miss Bertha."

"I have made a mistake," said Durgan.

"But only in telling me what you would have withheld, and what, it would appear, those for whom I have done everything have long withheld—the one thing that it most behoved me to know." The lawyer stopped in his walk, and spoke shaken with distress. "I will admit to you, Mr. Durgan, that for years I have been aware that my clients withheld something from me; I may say 'bitterly aware,' for, the trial being over, I could not with delicacy renew my questions. But I believed in their integrity, and have assured myself that their secret must be unimportant. You can estimate how acute is my present distress when I perceive that this concealment has covered what was the vital point, the clue to the murderer."

"I had no intention of telling you anything they did not tell you, Mr. Alden. At the same time, no one would be more glad than myself if they could emerge from the shadow of this mystery. But I think, as I said to you at the beginning, that unless you obtain Miss Claxton's permission to act further, you ought to leave the matter in her hands. You must trust to her good sense and good feeling."

Durgan had paused at his own turning;

Alden went a few steps further and faced round, hat in hand. Under the trees, in the glimmer of the summer night, his jaded attitude and unkempt hair were just seen and no more. He looked, indeed, like a storm-tossed soul, already in the shades of some nether world. Even then he summoned up all that he might of his precise manner.

"My dear sir—my dear sir! I have had more experience of such matters than you, and much more knowledge of this most distressing and mysterious case. I thank you for your advice. I thank you. I must act according to my own conscience."

CHAPTER XXVII

IT was that season in the summer when, in regions remote from fields of harvest, time itself stands still. Nothing is doing in the wild wood. Each young thing is fledged and flown, or, strong in its coat of fur, is off and away; the flower of the season is passed, the berry hangs green on the bush. The sky is empty; the earth is dry. The panting trees of the valleys speak to the trees of the mountains, telling them, in hot, dry whispers, to look out for the autumn that comes from afar. Only sometimes, in the morning on the hill-tops, a courier comes from the season that tarries. With feet that trip on the nodding weeds, and a voice singing in the fluttering trees, and a smile that speaks in a bluer sky, the unseen courier of autumn comes and goes. The hearts of men and beasts are excited, they know not why, and the berry and the grape and the tender leaf turn red.

Such was the weather in which the time of waiting passed.

Within two days Bertha passed down the road twice on village errands. Her horse each time loitered as it passed the mine until Durgan at last went out and walked a few steps by her bridle. He was afraid to talk with her lest he should say more, or less, or something quite different from what he would wish to say. But Bertha would speak.

"Mr. Durgan, are you still quite sure? I cannot tell you how you have lightened my heart, but I must hear it again. It came to you freshly the other night; after thinking it over, are you still quite sure?"

"Of what?" he asked. He could not think of anything connected with Bertha's misfortunes of which he was sure at all.

"That it could not have been as I thought— that my dear sister——"

"Your sister has no mental weakness; and she did not commit that crime," he said almost sharply. "If that is what you mean, I am as sure of it as that I stand here."

"Don't be angry with me. You speak so severely. But I can't tell you how I like to hear you say it."

"It was a bugbear of your own imagination, and I feel angry with you when I think of it. And if you take my advice you will never, never under any circumstances, let her, or anyone else, know that you thought such a thing."

"I would rather tell her all about it sometime. She would forgive it."

"I dare say she would." Durgan spoke bitterly. "I don't know what forgiveness in such a case is; but no doubt, whatever it is, it would cost her more than you can conceive. She would give it to you; but you are a child if you think that she would ever recover from the wound of such knowledge. God may put such things right in the next life, but never in this. That, at least, is my opinion."

"I am offended with you," she said. She was looking very well that day. Her blue cotton riding-dress and blue sun-bonnet well displayed the warm colour and youthful contour of her face. There was a peace in her eyes, too, that he had never seen there before. "I wanted to tell you something else, but you have made me angry."

"Forgive me, then. It is so easy." There was sarcasm in his voice.

236 THE EARTHLY PURGATORY

She thought for a few minutes, and seemed to forget her quarrel.

"Mr. Alden went to Hilyard, and he has come back without finding out anything about 'Dolphus. I was so much afraid. I have asked Hermie if we might not tell him just about 'Dolphus; but she spoke to me so solemnly, so sadly, that now I only regret that I told *you*. I want to beg you never to repeat it. I don't understand Hermie's motives, but I can't side against her."

"What has Alden been doing?"

"He has been attending to business letters and papers. He is making this his holiday, but of course he has always a great deal of business on hand. He thinks a great deal over his writing. This morning he spent hours pacing in the pasture and sitting on the stile."

"Ah!" said Durgan.

"He actually came in with his necktie crooked, he was thinking so hard," continued Bertha. "He is good, but I can't think why Hermie cares for him so; he usually looks so like a doll."

In a few minutes Durgan dropped the bridle and turned back. His mind was uneasy.

But the next afternoon Bertha descended in a

different mood. She had evidently been watching to see his negro labourers depart, for she stood on the rock ledge before they were out of sight.

"You told him my secret. How could you? You promised at least not to tell till you had spoken to me. You never explained yesterday that you had told. Oh, how he has turned against us! And you! There is no one in the world we can trust."

Durgan stood in awkward distress before her. His intention not to tell could not balance his stupidity in having betrayed anything.

"I told you because you said you must know my story on Adam's account, but you found Adam's safety provided for; you said you must know lest you should do injustice to 'Dolphus, but he will likely die before the trial comes on; and yet you have babbled to Mr. Alden, not being able to keep faith with a most unhappy woman for a few days. I was foolish, I was wrong, to tell you our secret; but you forced me to speak. Oh, how could you call yourself a gentleman and betray me so?"

She was very imperious, very handsome; but she was far too sad and frightened to be really angry.

As he stood before her without a word, con-

trition written on his face, she took shelter in
the threshold of his hut and, sitting by the open
door, began to cry piteously, not with abandon-
ment, but with the quietude of a real sorrow.

She spoke again. "Mr. Alden is a hound,
with his keen nose on a scent. He will not lift
it off till his victim is at bay. When I said to
Hermie that Mr. Alden would not rest now till
whoever did it was hanged, she fainted. She
was so ill upstairs in our room that I was
terrified, but she would not let Mr. Alden
know."

"Yes, but *who is* the victim ?"

She looked up suddenly. "He said you told
him who it is; and that I had told you. Hermie
never betrayed any feeling when he told her—it
was afterwards—but I know her heart is breaking."

"I am at my wit's end," said Durgan sadly.

"He says Hermie, my own Hermie, has made
every sacrifice to protect this Charlton Beardsley.
It is not true. There was no one she despised
and disliked so much. Whatever else is or is
not true, that is. Do I not know ? Did I not
see her even quarrel with our dear father about
this man because he had pretended to give
messages from mother ?" At this recollection

she wept again, her head in her hands. "My dear, dear father," she whispered. "Oh, if he could come back to us ! If he could only come back ! "

Durgan stood helpless. That faculty by which words arise unbidden in the mind kept obstinately repeating in Durgan's the name Charlton Beardsley in that tone of almost tender compassion given to it by Miss Claxton when he last spoke to her.

At last Bertha rose to go. "There is no such thing as truth," she cried. "I was false to Hermie in telling you what I did ; you were false to me. Mr. Alden is a false friend to us all. There is no truth."

Durgan laid a detaining hand on her arm. "Look up," he said.

She looked up at the dog-wood tree whose spring blossom had first cheered that rocky spot for Durgan. Across the unutterable brightness of the sky the tree held its horizontal sprays of golden leaves. The blue-bird of the south, dashed with gloss of crimson and green, pecked at the scarlet berries. The tree glistened in the light of evening. Above and beyond it the sky was radiant with the level light.

"Very probably there is no such thing as the

truth you seek in this world," he said ; " but
there must be truth somewhere, or why should
we all try to approximate to it, and feel so like
whipped dogs when we have failed ? "

For two or three days after that Durgan heard
nothing, but Alden came and went on the mountain road, and once again made the journey to
Hilyard.

At last, one evening after dark, Durgan
received a message demanding his presence at
the summit house. He went and found the
little family in some formal condition of distress
—the elder lady sitting calm but very sad, her
usually busy hands idle in her lap ; Bertha, her
face swollen with tears, sitting beside her sister
in an attitude of defiant protection ; Alden
moving restlessly about, his face blanched and
haggard. The weather over all the mountain
was still tense and dry. The cold had come
without rain—a highly nervous condition for the
human frame.

It was only Miss Claxton who tried to make
Durgan's arrival more agreeable to him by a few
words of ordinary conversation.

Then Alden spoke. " I believe now that
yours was the right suspicion, Mr. Durgan.
Miss Claxton having declined to help me at all,

I resolved to ask you to be present while I tell her exactly what I suspect with regard to Charlton Beardsley. I would not have Miss Claxton without a protector while I am obliged to say and do what she tells me will make me her worst enemy. If so, it must be so. I cannot be silent. I cannot be inactive. I cannot be responsible for a murderer's freedom. But I will do no more without giving you all fair warning. I believe your wife to be implicated. We are here agreed in desiring your presence."

Durgan looked at the women. How often had he seen them here in the mellow lamplight, at peace in this beautiful retreat.

Bertha looked up at him. "Stay with us," said she. "You have done us an injury by betraying my confidence; now ward off the consequences if you can."

Miss Claxton's gentle face was also upturned. "It is right that you should stay to know what accusation will be brought against your wife; but I do not need your protection."

She looked towards Alden when she had spoken, and Durgan saw the little man quiver with distress.

Durgan sat down beside the sisters.

R

CHAPTER XXVIII

ALDEN began with a stiff quaint bow to his little audience. It was easy to see that he had fallen into the mannerism of a court. "In making my statement it is not necessary for me to tell from what source I obtained any part of my information, or what is inference from information. I will say exactly what I now suppose to have happened upon the morning of the day on which Mr. Claxton was killed with unparalleled brutality, and his wife shot."

Durgan felt rebellion in its keenest form at this beginning, but sat in silence.

When Alden had once begun it was obvious that he felt the relief of open speech. He told in detail how he believed 'Dolphus to have been sent to Mr. Claxton's with a note announcing Beardsley's visit, which caused Miss Hermione to send the maids and Miss Bertha out of the house.

"But how," asked Alden, "did Beardsley come

to the house without observation ? I have found again and again that the thing that is hardest to detect has been done in the simplest and most obvious way. Negative evidence is often no evidence at all ; and the thing done most openly more often escapes remark than an attempt at secrecy. In this case two neighbours saw the maids go out on their errand; one saw the dark-faced boy enter. She swore he was an Italian music-boy, while in fact he was a mulatto. The servant of a neighbour said she saw the boy leave the house again. They both agreed that he was long and lanky. Everyone else in the neighbour-hood, with a chance of seeing, testified that no boy came or went. I believe that Beardsley came, as the boy came, in an open way, and was admitted by Miss Hermione. Again, one neigh-bour swears that she saw the two maids go down the street together ; another, that only one went down alone while she was looking. Cross-examined, she could not be sure whether the one maid she saw was the cook, or housemaid, or charwoman, but only that she came out of the Claxton house. The other neighbours had not seen any woman leave the house. This shows what such evidence is worth. I believe Beardsley left the house disguised in the clothes of the boy. The boy was almost grown, Beardsley not large. No doubt, being in the habit of personating spirits and juggling, escape would be no difficulty to him. I am still unable to suggest any motive for the crime." Alden paused.

"Go on." The words were spoken breathlessly by Bertha.

Alden went on solemnly. "I think, Hermione, you knew the boy's message to be from Beardsley. You must have admitted Beardsley to the house, Hermione! In the night you helped the boy to escape. It is not possible that you did not know that Beardsley had committed the crime. I am convinced that you helped him also to escape. One possible explanation of your action, and the subsequent concealment, is that he extracted some oath of secrecy which you wrongly considered binding."

There was a breathless silence.

"But I think you have too much good sense to consider such a compulsory promise binding. You have had another reason."

There was still silence.

"The fact that you did not denounce him points to the fact that you helped Beardsley's escape. The fact that you sent the mulatto to Mrs. Durgan's address proves that you knew where Beardsley had taken refuge. Beardsley went to Mrs. Durgan's house, not to his former lodgings. She must have known that some disaster had happened if he returned in disguise; she must quickly have known from the papers the extent of his guilt. She certainly had him in her house ill a week after—really very ill, for Mr. Durgan, on one of his rare visits, found two hospital nurses attending him. It was said to be a severe case of pleurisy with complications; and he has been, or has pretended to be, more or less of an invalid ever since. But before his illness he acted his part well. He certainly held his séances regularly for a number of evenings after the crime. I made very strict inquiry at the time of several members of this circle as to its nature, because of the connection Mr. Claxton had with it. Beardsley went into his trances, and spoke with strange tongues, and what not, during that week. I knew this because several of his disciples, who believed in his dealings with the unseen world, tried to call up the spirits of Mr. and Mrs. Claxton, so unhappily departed, and entreated for some information as to their murderer. The villain had not the hardihood to personate his own victims."

Alden paused suddenly, and demanded of

the sisters, "You remember hearing of the incident?"

Bertha, her face flushed and excited, gave a hasty "Yes." Miss Claxton made an indifferent motion of assent. She preserved a uniform expression of great sadness. She seemed to take hardly any special interest in anything said.

"This boy, 'Dolphus, went also straight to Mrs. Durgan's house. He has been sheltered by Beardsley and Mrs. Durgan; he has been Beardsley's valet ever since. Mrs. Durgan may have hid them both in the first instance out of pity; or she, too, may have had another reason. She would fear to send them away later lest her connivance in their hiding should become known."

"Consider," said Durgan. "Do you think my wife, or any other woman, would voluntarily live in daily terror of being killed by such a madman as you describe?"

"Is there no adequate motive that you can suggest?" Alden returned.

"Love," said he. "But I am certain that my wife has not been in love."

Hermione Claxton looked at Durgan for a moment; a tinge of colour, and an abatement of her sorrow were evident. Then she relapsed into her former attitude.

Alden stood in front of her, watching her changing expression with impassioned eagerness. "In the name of God, Hermione," he cried solemnly, "why do you shield this man? Why do you still wish to shield him? Why are you glad that Mr. Durgan should believe that love does not exist between him and Mrs. Durgan?"

His sudden manner of agonised affection, and words that came like a cry from the heart, brought a hush of trembling expectation. Bertha gazed intently at her sister, unconscious of the tears of excitement that were running over her own eyes. Durgan, who had never thought to see Alden so moved, felt the utmost wonder. But the fragile, faded woman, to whom the passionate question had been addressed, faced her questioner with no other change in the calm front she bore than an added degree of sadness.

"Hermione," cried Alden again, "why did you conceal this man's guilt from me at the time, and why do you still wish to conceal it?"

"Herbert," she replied very gently, "you have no evidence of his guilt."

"I have," he replied.

Durgan felt himself start nervously. Such a statement from this keen legal mind was like a declaration of proof.

The effect of the words upon Miss Hermione was a visible shudder which ran through her frame.

"Evidence?" she said, as if still doubting; but terror was written on her face.

"Two days ago I went to Hilyard at the summons of the doctor and constable. The coloured prisoner, called Adolphus Courthope, was supposed to be dying, and desired to see me. When I went, he asked me to take down a confession and a statement, parts of which supplied links in the story I have told you. The doctor was witness to the interview. Courthope swore that Beardsley was the criminal."

Miss Claxton looked at him steadily. "What reason have you to assume that what he said is true?"

"In all those parts where I can test its truth it appears to be true. He referred me to Bertha for the fact that she aided his escape at night."

"Birdie will not corroborate that. She will tell you nothing."

"He would hardly have asked her to corroborate a lie," said Alden. "He told me that when in New York he knew he was dying, his conscience caused him to bring some documents which he believed to incriminate Beardsley; that he gave them to you by appointment on the night of Eve's death; that after giving them he discovered that Adam's wife had been spying on the interview and had followed you up the hill. She showed him a certain place where she saw you hide these letters. He added, in the most matter-of-fact way, that he then killed Eve for her treachery to you, and because she would only make mischief."

Bertha stood up in great wrath. "How can you say that my sister did such things as this? No word of this is true. How can you believe a man who is a murderer?"

Alden went on looking at Hermione. "I went to the tree of which he gave me a rough drawing."

He took from his coat two packets of old letters, with their wrapping of oil-silk, which he had unfastened.

"I have read them," he said. "I did not wish to do so without your permission and that of Mr. Durgan, as they chiefly belong to his wife; but it was necessary, and the fact that I found them there, and also their contents, prove the most unlikely part of his tale to be true— that you have trafficked secretly with such a man as he, and crept out at night to meet him and hide documents which——" He paused half-way through the sentence ; his voice broke, and the tremor coming at so strong a moment, brought all the little gracious ways of his long friendship and service for Hermione to their minds. The strange scene vibrated with a throb of sorrow.

"Herbert," she said falteringly, "you have indeed become my enemy, concerting with this poor wretch to outwit me, spying upon my most private actions."

"Nay, Hermione ; I did not even ask the man for his evidence. I was forced, in the name of common justice, and above all, of justice to you, to hear it ; and I am justified in what I have done since, because I have done it to save you from yourself."

"I beg your pardon," said she. "For a moment I spoke unjustly ; but, whatever your motives, you have become my enemy. Those letters were stolen by a servant to injure a master who, whatever else his faults, had treated him with unvarying kindness. They were given to me under the mistaken idea that I could use them for my own advantage. I cannot ; nor can you."

"I read them, Hermione, because, without

suspicion and by mere accident, I had read your telegram to Charlton Beardsley the other day."

She rose up now. There was a movement of her small clasped hands, as though she wrung them together.

"When I read it at the post-office, merely to aid in its transmission, I saw its significance only too plainly. I withheld it for a day. Then I had it sent by an agent whom I could trust, and whom I instructed to watch the house of the recipient. I could not have connived at the man's escape. Had he tried to get away after receiving your wire, I should have been justified in his arrest."

"Did you have my message sent from Hilyard?" she asked suddenly.

"No. From New York. But it was the exact message."

She was white to the lips. "It had no significance coming from New York." She lifted both hands with a gesture of despair.

Instinctively he chose quick words to comfort her. "No, you wanted to warn him against coming here! But Beardsley had gone. I suppose he had got some other warning. He had fled three days before. My men could gain no information."

She was comforted. Some colour returned to her face.

Alden spoke out once more. "In Heaven's name, what motive have you for seeking this man's freedom ? Why hide these letters ? They are written between Beardsley and Mrs. Durgan. What secret of yours can they contain ?"

She looked at him with unutterable pain in her face, but gave no word or sound.

"Hermione !" he cried ; "this trickster had only been a few months upon this continent when this crime was committed ; and during those few months you gave me to understand that I was your dearest and only intimate friend. We were together constantly ; we were looking forward to marriage. It cannot be possible that, at that same time, you contracted a friendship—shall I say an affection ?—for this man ? You spoke of him to me as a person whose pretensions you despised, whose slight acquaintance with your father you deplored ; and, beyond this, you told me that you had never seen him. Am I to believe that, in spite of all this, he was your lover ?"

"My lover !" She repeated the word with white lips, and remained gazing at him for some minutes as if paralysed with surprise. Then with a gesture of that dignity which only a mind innocent in thought and act can command, she rose and turned away, with no further word, toward the staircase that led from the room.

"You know that is not true," cried Bertha to Alden fiercely. She stood up as a man would who was ready to make good the word with a blow. Then she called, "Hermione! Hermione! Come back. Don't you see that Mr. Alden has no choice but to give this Beardsley up to justice, and hand over all the evidence he has in these letters to the police?"

Hermione turned to Alden again. "Is that true? Do not deceive me in the hope of making me confess anything; but tell me truly, do not say you have no choice."

But he could not abandon the point which gave him such unbounded astonishment. "What motive have you for protecting him? Why do you love him?—for you do love him, Hermione."

"I am asking you whether it is no longer in my power to protect him, should I wish to do so."

"Oh, my dear; give me some notion why you want to save him."

The term of affection, if not used between them for the first time, was certainly now first used before others. A slow flush mantled her faded, sensitive face.

"Alas! Herbert; is it not clear now why I should have kept my secret from you, if your conscience is such that you can concede no mercy to a criminal? You may be right. You may have no choice but to wield the law, and the law only. But if I had a choice, you cannot blame me for not telling you, who admit you have none. Do you not know that I have loved you —you only? Do you think I could have endured to be separated from you for a slight or a low motive, for a whim, or for a duty about which I felt the slightest doubt? And nothing has taken away the need for my silence. I cannot tell you my motive, or give you any indication whether the clue you now hold is true or false, or whether these letters will help you to do justice or lead you astray, or why I went out to get them at night, or why I put them where Bertha would not have found them in the event of my death. I put these letters where I could find them should a certain contingency arise in my life, and where, failing that, they would be lost. I will not tell you more, or give you leave to use them."

"Hermione!" cried Bertha, the energy of a

long distress in her tone, "for my sake, can you not help us to understand? I have tried to be brave; and if you will not tell, I will stand by you in anything; but my courage is all gone now. I cannot bear this mystery and disgrace."

The elder sister looked at her with tenderness and pity. It was a lingering look that a mother might cast on a child doomed to a crippled life. But she gave no answer, and went up the stairs.

CHAPTER XXIX

ALDEN looked at Bertha. "Mr. Durgan must read these letters," he said, "because they belong to his wife. You must choose whether you will be a witness to the reading. Yours is a filial as well as a sisterly part. It is in the effort to bring your father's enemy to justice that I take this step. On the other hand, you may think that your sister has also acted with that filial duty in view, and that, in taking a course in opposition to her wishes, you would be casting a reflection upon her conduct which is disloyal. I cannot advise you, you must judge for yourself."

Bertha did not speak.

"The course which your sister has pursued appears to me suicidal," continued Alden. "I cannot, if I would, endorse her action further; but you must judge for yourself."

"Whatever duty to my dear father I leave unperformed, his happiness cannot now be

256

marred. I only wish to serve my sister now."

Then she followed her sister upstairs.

When Alden was relieved from constraint, his face and figure settled into lines even more haggard and weary than before.

"I will give you the letters in the order of their dates," said he to Durgan.

The letters were carefully arranged. He had made notes concerning each on a slip of paper.

The first was written upon cheap notepaper in a cramped hand. Durgan, as he read, character-ised the writer as a half-educated person, unac-customed to social usage. It was dated from New York, and on a day about a month before the Claxton tragedy. It ran thus :—

"Mrs. Durgan.

"Madame,—I find the boarding-house to which you have been so good as to recommend me very comfortable. The parcel of comforts has reached and been duly received by me, for which also kindly receive my thanks. But I cannot forbear from reminding you that he who would seek spiritual knowledge and communion with those in a finer state of being than our own, must eschew such unnecessary gratification

s

of the flesh. Again thanking you, dear madame,

> "I remain, your obedient servant,
> "JOHN CHARLTON BEARDSLEY."

Durgan turned this over and over. There was no post-mark or stamp on the envelope. It had perhaps been returned by the bearer of the parcel referred to. The paper was not soiled, and the fragrance of his wife's own stationery adhered to it. She had evidently kept this paltry note among her own papers until recently —why? A fashionable woman must receive hundreds of such notes. Then, too, to keep what was of no use was not in accordance with his wife's business habits.

After this followed three more notes on the same paper. They also were brief and formal, giving thanks for favours, making or cancelling engagements to teach spiritual lore.

Then came one dated the day before the Claxton murder. Durgan felt a strange thrill as he read it :—

> "MADAME,—I feel compelled to visit Mr. Claxton at his own residence to-morrow. I feel that it is my duty to declare to him in the presence of Mrs. Claxton—or if he will

not consent to this, to warn Mr. Claxton of the risk to his soul which he encounters in his present meetings with———"

Here a line had been carefully erased. The next line began in the middle of a sentence.

"———not think that I have any other than an honourable intention. For again I say that if we seek to know the spirit world we must purge ourselves of all dross.

"I am, your obedient servant,

"JOHN CHARLTON BEARDSLEY."

"This is of importance," said Durgan. "He intended to go to the house on the fatal day, and there is suggestion of material for a quarrel over some unknown person—a woman, probably, as Mrs. Claxton's presence is required."

"Is there reason to assume this third person unknown? It may have been a name that is erased, or it may have been a pronoun in the second person. Shall we read on?"

The next letter was dated the day after the crime. It ran :—

"MRS. DURGAN,

"Madame,—I am sensible of kindness in your inquiries about my health. I have, as you are aware, received a great shock in hearing of the terrible fate of our friend, Mr. Claxton. Alas! In the midst of life we are in death. I had, as you know, held the intention of paying him a call upon that very day, but, instead, fell into a trance soon after my simple breakfast of bread and milk. In that trance I saw the dark deed committed, but could not see the actor. The terror of the hour has preyed upon my health. If I can keep my evening engagements this week it will be all that I can do. I will not see you again at present, except in public.

"Your obedient servant,

"J. C. B."

"Do you think he could possibly have gone out and done it in his trance, and never known his own guilt?" asked Durgan.

"Observe that that letter appears to be written from Beardsley's, while 'Dolphus swears that he was then in Mrs. Durgan's house."

The next was a reply from Mrs. Durgan, upon the costly, scented paper her husband knew so well—crest and monogram and address embossed in several delicate colours. It was dated the same day.

"DEAR MR. CHARLTON BEARDSLEY,—I am sorry indeed to hear that your health has been too greatly strained by spiritual exercises and (may I not say?) by too great abstinence. I regret this on my own account, for I am deprived of the valuable instruction you have been giving me in spiritual matters. I confess I cannot glean so much wisdom from you when I meet you only in the more public séance. But on no account risk any danger to your health.

" Yours cordially,

"ANNA DURGAN.

" P.S.—I was so absorbed in my personal disappointment that I have forgotten to express my horror and sympathy at the terrible news (which is now in all the papers) concerning your friend, Mr. Claxton, and his family."

Next, with the same date, came another note from Mrs. Durgan, briefly inviting the medium to pay a week's visit at her house, and stating that an old nurse of her own would wait on him if he preferred to keep his room.

The next letter was dated two months later, and was from Beardsley at Atlantic City. In it the patient recounted with gratitude all the attention he had received during a long illness suffered in Mrs. Durgan's house. He also spoke of much pleasure in a further friendship with her, and the hope of spending his life not far from her. More elegance of thought and language was now displayed.

After this there were several other letters, written at intervals during the next year, alternately by Beardsley and Mrs. Durgan, and filled only with matters of ordinary friendship—discussions on spiritualism, and of a plan that Beardsley should avail himself permanently of Mrs. Durgan's hospitality. Beardsley stated that he had no longer the health to continue his work as a medium.

When the reading was finished, and Alden was waiting, Durgan was loth to speak. He felt a curious sense of helplessness. Why had these particular letters been kept ? Was it to incriminate Charlton Beardsley or to exculpate him ? The period of the letters was well chosen with reference to the crime, but how had his wife been able to foresee a month before the murder that she might want to produce the notes of that date? Then arose a question of much greater interest to Durgan. The Beardsley revealed in these letters was, as he had always believed, the last man to attract Mrs. Durgan. If innocent, he appeared to be a simple-minded, uneducated enthusiast in bad health and liable to fits. If guilty, there was still less reason why a woman whose motive was always selfish, and whose aim was ambitious, should compromise herself by befriending him.

"What do you think of these letters?" asked Durgan impatiently.

Alden gave a little genteel snort of anger and annoyance. He looked towards the stairs and spoke in a low voice. "I confide in you, Mr. Durgan. In confidence, I may say I am confounded. The world has said that this was an extraordinary case, and that without knowing this latest and most baffling development. I confess I am confounded."

"But you will have some theory about them?"

"The only thing they prove is that someone has thought it worth while to try to deceive someone else; and I should think—pardon me—that the agent in the matter is Mrs. Durgan. This is her writing, is it not?"

"Yes."

"Beardsley's letters are all forgeries except one."

Durgan took back the letters to seek evidence of forgery. His hand trembled.

"Don't you see which is the genuine one?" asked Alden.

Durgan did not see until it was pointed out to him that the letter which contained the erasure differed from the rest in displaying some peculiarities of crude handwriting which were more or less successfully copied, but exaggerated, in the others which bore his supposed signature.

"Do you agree with me that my wife's are genuine?" asked Durgan haughtily.

"I have no reason to suppose otherwise. They are all in the same hand, but I think——"

"Go on," said Durgan.

"I think they were not written at the dates given, but were composed to make up this series."

"Do you suppose, then, that my wife is the author of these Beardsley forgeries?"

"I cannot tell. If they were written in Beardsley's interest, why did he not write them himself? But if not in his interest, whoever forged them must have done it at her bidding."

As Durgan kept silence, Alden spoke again.

" I ought to explain to you, perhaps with an apology, why I suggested that the person referred to in the erased line may have been Mrs. Durgan. By mere accident I heard, a year after the trial, a piece of gossip which first made me pitch on that one letter as probably genuine. I am loth to mention it to you, for it appeared to be trivial talk about a mere mistake. A man who had belonged to that somewhat secret circle of Beardsley's was telling me that Beardsley knew nothing of society, and was, like all lower-class men, at first quite unaccustomed to the idea of mere friendship between men and women, and, as an illustration of this, he went on to say what I am referring to. Mrs. Durgan and Claxton seemed to have discovered some spiritual affinity. The spirits, I understood, sometimes spoke through Mrs. Durgan and sent messages to him——"

" She said they did ? "

" Personally, of course, I don't believe in such communications, but we may believe that Mrs. Durgan believed——"

' " I was not entering into that question. I merely wish to be clear as to what occurred."

" Yes ; I understood that Mrs. Durgan said they sent messages of an agreeable and flattering

nature ; and Beardsley suspected that, they were
not genuine, and, being a person of primitive
ideas, showed disapproval. He thought they
indicated undue interest in Claxton on Mrs.
Durgan's part. The man told me that all who
knew of the incident laughed at Beardsley's lack
of knowledge of the world. He gave me to
understand no one thought the incident of any
importance, and all had the good feeling not to
speak of it after poor Claxton's death."

"Did they suppose Beardsley to be jealous ? "

"Not at all. My informant, a man of the
world, represented him as having the idea that a
high moral tone was necessary to ensure the
success of his entertainments, and that these
flattering messages were not in harmony with
such a tone."

"You heard this a year ago and no suspicion
of Beardsley entered your mind ? "

"No. How should it ? My informant ended
his chat by remarking how well Mrs. Durgan
knew how to disarm criticism, for, instead of being offended, she had most charitably supported
the simple moralist during years of ill health."

"It is easy to be wise after the event," said
Durgan ; and then he asked, "What are you
going to do now ? "

"The chief thing we have got to consider is that, although these letters, and above all, those I have not yet shown you, confirm the mulatto's tale that Beardsley was at the house, we have as yet no explanation whatever of the crime, and no reason whatever to accuse Beardsley of it beyond the fact that he was there. I do not see how to get further except by discovering a clue to Miss Claxton's conduct. The kernel of the secret lies there."

"I see quite clearly," rejoined Durgan, "that we are, as you say, far from any explanation of the mystery; but as far as my wife is concerned, these letters appear to me to show that she knew that she was protecting this man at the risk of danger to herself. She has prepared this series to save herself if he is found out. The one letter which you suppose to be his is evidence that he had the intention of visiting the Claxtons that morning; the rest of the letters only imply that she believed he had never gone. If, as we now suppose, the cause of quarrel between Beardsley and poor Claxton was this misapprehension of his regarding my wife's feeling for Claxton, she may have sheltered him at first to save scandal involving herself."

"Yet," said Alden, "we must admit that this

does not appear to be any sufficient motive for Mrs. Durgan's conduct. We agree that only some important fact, as yet unknown to us, can explain the action of these two women."

Alden put down his notes on the small table. They sat in silence. The smouldering birch log in the stove chimney emitted only an occasional spit of flame. The dogs slumbered in front of it. The shaded lamp, which Durgan had often regarded as the symbol of domestic felicity, threw the same soft light around the graceful room as on the first evening of his introduction to it. Upstairs there was an occasional sound made by the movements of the sisters, which gave a soft reminder of their presence in the house, and no more. Through the low, uncurtained windows the mountain trees and the meadows were seen outlined in the starlight, as on the night of his arrival.

"What of these other letters you still have in your hand?" said Durgan at last.

"There are three that were tied up and hidden, evidently before the stolen packet came into her possession; and three that were with the rest that you have seen. These last three I cannot let you see. They are the saddest letters I have ever read. They are written to Charlton, and although without date or signature, undoubtedly in Miss Claxton's writing. They implore him by every sacred feeling of love and duty to turn to God in repentance and accept the Christian salvation. Mr. Durgan, nothing but love and the most earnest sense of duty could have prompted these letters, and I wish, in your presence, to put them in the fire. They have been rejected and spurned by the cur to whom they were sent, and although they are undoubted proofs that for him she has felt the madness—I can call it by no other word—the madness of love, they shall never be used as evidence against her."

The little man stepped forward and laid them on the fire. The tears, unfelt, fell from his eyes as he did so. The flame shot up from the glowing log, and the dark, uncurtained windows of the room repeated the quivering light.

The sorrow of it drowned Durgan's curiosity. He forgot to wonder what letters Miss Claxton had previously hidden in the tree till Alden roused himself to speak again.

"The three letters still left, which apparently came months ago, at intervals, in response to those just burnt, are addressed to Miss Claxton at my office. I judge from this that Beardsley never knew of the alias 'Smith' or of this retreat. Indeed, Adolphus told me he does not know." Alden paused absently.

"And these letters?" Durgan reminded.

"These letters are no doubt from that beast. They are in feigned hand and anonymous; and the subject is money—no religion, no duty, no affection, is to be believed as long as money is withheld. Thousands of dollars are demanded. I've no means of knowing whether this money was given or not."

Durgan went over the notes, which Alden had described accurately.

"The negro is really dying, I suppose?" he asked. "He can help us no further?"

"Yes; he may be dead by this time; but, curiously enough, to the end of my interview he was chuckling, and saying that he would pay the villain and right the lady yet. But he would not give me, or the doctor, any indication of what he meant. He adjured me to——"

"Listen." Durgan went to the window as he spoke, and the dogs pricked their ears.

"I hear nothing," said Alden.

"I ought to be going home," said Durgan. "What were you saying?"

"Only that the fellow told me to keep my

wits about me, and tell you to do the same. There is something to be subtracted from all the evidence he gave, for he was certainly, if rational at all, in a very fantastic humour."

The lawyer's tones were low and weary. Durgan was not even listening. He had opened the window a little.

"I think there is a horse, or horses, on the road from the Cove," he said. His thought glanced back to the last time he heard horsemen approach in the night, to arrest Adam. No errand of less baneful import seemed to fit the circumstances now.

The French clock on the mantelshelf rang out twelve musical strokes.

CHAPTER XXX

THERE is, perhaps, no more enthralling sound than the far but sure approach of someone who comes unlooked-for to a lonely place. The two men who were keeping vigil became certain that travellers were ascending the steep zigzags of Deer. They looked at one another in apprehensive silence, and went softly out to that side of the house nearest the road. The young moon had set, and there was cloud overhead. Almost an hour's journey below them the creak of wheel, the sound of hoof, came faint but nearer. The two house dogs stood by the men, a growl in their throats.

Bertha came downstairs and out to them, a shawl over her head. The mountain nights had been growing colder; the air was bleak and dry.

"Hermie is terribly ill," she said. "She has cried till the pain in her head is anguish—and who can possibly be coming?"

Then she turned indignantly to Alden. "Is this some plan of your arranging?"

Alden denied in dispirited tones, and suggested that perhaps some travellers had lost their way.

"People don't usually climb a mountain by mistake," she retorted.

"There are two horses—and two men talking —and wheels," said Durgan, slowly reckoning up the sounds he heard.

"Go in, and take the dogs," said Alden to Bertha. "We will go down to the mine and meet them, so that Hermione need not be disturbed."

"You need not be so careful to protect her now," she said hardly. "She is in too great pain to care what happens."

Then Durgan was striding down the trail, and Alden hopping nimbly over the rocks beside him.

"The last visitors who rode here through the night brought handcuffs," said Durgan grimly.

He could not divest himself of the idea that some armed fate was close upon them all.

He lit his lantern, and kindled a fire of sticks in the stove of his hut. Alden, who was shivering with cold, warmed himself. The travellers were now resting their horses a half-mile below.

T

The keen air, the new excitement, were a spur to the mind of the weary lawyer. He began to talk with renewed melancholy, and a persistence that wearied Durgan's ears.

" So far, we are not only without proof, but without reasonable hypothesis. The cleverest detective in New York tells me that Beardsley left New York and cannot be traced. When we find him, we shall only have, as means to incriminate him, the word of a dead negro, whose mind was obviously failing when he gave his evidence, and one letter which——"

Durgan's impatience was intolerable. He went out on to the dark road. He thought of that other night, gorgeous in its whiteness, when the full moon had looked down on the beautiful bronze form of the murdered woman and on a strolling, dandified valet, of whose portrait Durgan remembered every detail. He had seen him in the glamour of the silvered avenue ; and his silken hair and long whiskers, the expanse of shirt-front, the flash of false jewels, and his mad utterance, which was now gradually taking the form of truth, lived again in his memory. He remembered, too, the crimson dawn in which he had witnessed Adam's passionate grief, and his own rage of indignation when the next night had brought with it, on this same road, the worst of insults to taint that grief.

The cause of all that coil of evil and pain had been the quiet lady, whom they had just left with the intense loneliness of her secret, shut off in her anguish from sister and lover. For her sake, it seemed, Eve had been killed, and Adam had wept, and the vain serving-man had used his last vital powers to save her 'from a world's reproach. As yet there was no outcome of it all, except dissension and misery.

The horses below began to move again. Durgan went in to Alden. They sometimes heard a thin, impatient voice raised high in questioning tones, and answers given. When the horses had passed the last turn below, the words of the thin voice could be heard clearly.

"Drivah, what is this light?" There was a slight drawl and an assumption of importance.

"I think I have heard that voice before," said the lawyer slowly, listening; "but I cannot tell where."

"Is this the top of the mountain, drivah? Is this the house?"

"I can't be sure, but I think I know it," commented the lawyer again. "Do you recognise it?"

"No, I do not."

Durgan stood out on the road.

"Then drive on. If this is not the summit house, drive on, drivah. Don't stop." There was a note of alarm in the thin tone.

Durgan's lantern flashed its light upon horses and driver and old-fashioned surrey from the hotel at Hilyard. The driver was a silent man, well known on the road. Within, his keen, facile face bent forward in ill temper and alarm, sat an emaciated man, wrapped in a rich fur coat and propped with cushions.

The driver had so far answered in lazy monosyllables. Now, on recognising Durgan, he pulled up the carriage. The thin-voiced traveller addressed Durgan.

"I am going to the boarding-house of a Miss Smith. I understand there is a lawyer there, the best in the State. I will not detain you, sir. Go on, drivah ; we are much too late now."

The owner of the voice leaned back in the surrey. He was evidently alarmed by his surroundings ; but a stranger might well be excused for showing some dislike of the long, steep road, the extreme solitude, and the sudden appearance of a man who barred the way.

Durgan turned his light on the face of the

driver. "What's the meaning of this?" he asked sternly.

The man returned his inspection with a queer, sphinx-like look that had in it something of the nature of a grin and a wink, but gave no indication as to the cause of his humour. He grumbled as he clumsily tumbled off his seat. Then, opening the surrey door, he remarked, in a casual tone, that his horses could go no further.

"If this 'ere gentleman doesn't keep summer hotels and big-bug lawyers handy, I dunno anyone as does 'bout here. As for Miss Smith's house, we'll have a rest first."

Again the face of the invalid, keen and drawn by pain or passion, was thrust forward from the shadow of the carriage. His voice was shrill enough to sound at first like a shriek. "Look here, my man; you needn't suppose the money I've got to pay you is in my pockets. It's in Hilyard, where you'll get all the currency you want when you've done my work; but you'll gain nothing by stopping here."

On seeing Durgan more clearly he looked about him in absolute terror, grasping the rug that impeded his movements as if wondering only how to fling himself out of their reach, or else not knowing whether to argue or ingratiate.

The driver held the door, taking the volley of weak-voiced profanity in the passive way common to the region.

Durgan's amusement at the driver's mastery, and at being himself so obviously mistaken for a robber, was overlaid by astonishment and curiosity.

"I am working a small mica mine close by. You can come into my camp to rest and get warm if you wish to." He spoke to the agitated traveller in the low, haughty tone that usually won for him the immediate respect of those inferior in social position. But the traveller only answered in a more imperious tone.

"Who are you, sir? Is this Bear Mountain? I was told it was. This man," he cried, pointing to the driver, "engaged to bring me to a mountain called Bear and a house kept by a woman called Smith. We were delayed—horribly delayed—by one of the horses casting a shoe. I ask you, sir, what does this man mean by turning me out at a mica mine? What does he mean?"

"I should like to know," said Durgan. "You have evidently been misled."

The driver here left the open carriage door, and began busying himself about the harness.

Again suggesting that the traveller might take advantage of his fire if he chose, Durgan turned back to his camp.

Alden stood outside, unseen from the carriage in the black shadow of the hut. He had the baffled air of a hound who, thinking he has found a scent, loses it again. He shook his head; his eyes contracted in concentrated attention. "I've no idea who he is; but I think he is acting a part."

The stranger now proved himself a man of the world by descending from the carriage with some polite expressions of relief at obtaining rest from the intolerable road and gratitude for Durgan's hospitality.

He was of middle height, and stooped as he walked. His travelling coat was of the richest, the muffling of the fur collar and the slouch of the warm felt hat seemed habitual to him. In spite of them he shivered in the mountain night.

He went close to the fire, unbuttoned his coat to let the warmth reach him, and took out a card-case.

"Perhaps you will be good enough to extract a card," said he, handing it to Durgan. "My fingers are numb."

He took off his gloves, and chafed his hands

before the blaze. He took off his hat, holding its inside to the fire to warm. He had the appearance of a man of perhaps fifty, with face withered and sunburnt. His hair was black, his moustache waxed, his beard pointed. He looked like a fashion plate from Paris, handsome in his way, but his skin and eyes gave the impression of pain impatiently borne. The sense of being an aristocrat was written large all over him. His cat's-eye pin, the cutting of his seal ring, answered true to the glare of the firelight. Having shown himself, as it would appear accidentally, he put on his hat and buttoned up his collar.

Durgan took a card from a well-filled and well-worn card-case and read it aloud, "Mr. Adolphus Courthope." It gave as an address a club in New Orleans.

"I heard a few days ago that a namesake of mine, a scoundrelly fellow, whose mother was one of our niggers, is lying in jail at Hilyard, charged with murder. Of course, I have no responsibility for the fellow—never saw him till to-day. Still, his mother was my foster-sister, the daughter of the good old mammy who nursed me. She gave him my name, and— damn it—I don't care to have the fellow publicly hanged. Seems in a bad way now with lung trouble; but he'll revive—that's the way with these cases."

Durgan disliked this man, but was surprised to find that he pitied him still more. The terror that he had just shown, the illusive resemblance in his eyes to someone—perhaps someone more worthy of pity—the very disparity of physical size and strength, all inspired in Durgan an unreasoning instinct to protect him.

The other went on. "Only reached Hilyard to-day. The poor fellow would have it that there was a woman called Smith, who kept a small summer hotel, or something of the kind, located here, who alone could give the evidence that would get him off; and that there was a clever lawyer boarding with her who would take up the case on her evidence. Would ·have it there was nothing for it but for me to come straight on here. I'm not the man to give up what I've undertaken, but if I'd known what the roads were like, confound it if I'd not have stayed in New Orleans. I say this to you, sir, because I see you are a man of my own class— damn it, there are few enough of us left."

Certain now that this man had been sent by 'Dolphus, Durgan perceived that till now he had

had some vague hope that 'Dolphus, as some *deus ex machina*, would contrive to trick Beardsley himself into their power. The production of this man, beguiled hither by a lie, was evidently the mulatto's supreme effort ; but this man, whoever he was, was certainly not Charlton Beardsley, for however accomplished an actor he may be, Durgan felt certain he had never been a man of plebeian origin.

"Is there no hotel that I can sleep in to-night?" asked the other shortly. "Has that cursed nigger not told me the truth?"

"Not precisely. Had he any reason for endeavouring to mislead you?"

"Well, I should rather think not. Trial coming on in two days. If he had his senses about him, he'd go only the quickest road to success."

This sounded genuine.

"And the driver brought you all this way and did not enlighten you?" said Durgan.

"Great God!" cried the other. "What could they mean?" And in his tone vibrated returning fear.

"*I have* a friend here—the lawyer to whom you are sent ; and there *is* a Miss Smith living higher up, but it is a private house."

Again the stranger overcame the fear he had a second time betrayed. "Oh, thanks awfully. That is all that matters. Has your friend turned in for the night ? "

Aware that Alden had been looking and listening through the chinks of the hut, Durgan wandered out in a slow detour among the trees, and brought Alden back with him. When they entered, the stranger was not looking toward the door.

"This is Mr. Theodore Alden, of New York," said Durgan ; and although the visitor only appeared to indolently turn his head and bow, Durgan felt sure that his whole body started and shrank under the heavy folds of his long coat.

"Mr. Courthope has come," began Durgan, and then, with indifferent manner, he repeated the story of Mr. Courthope of New Orleans. He could see that Alden had as yet no scent.

"Are you aware," began Alden, "that the other negro apprehended for this murder is being protected by his late owner upon the same grounds ? It is not a usual proceeding ; I might almost say—speaking from a wide knowledge of the South since the war—a novel proceeding. To have it repeated is a novel coincidence."

There was a little silence in which Durgan and Alden both observed the stranger narrowly, and neither felt sure whether his pause was caused by the inattentive habits of illness, or whether he was silent from annoyance. It would appear to have been the first, for, after again warming his legs and again rubbing his hands before the blaze, he lifted his head as if he had just observed that he had not replied.

"I beg your pardon—a bad habit of mine, forgetting to answer. As to coincidence, it isn't coincidence at all. My nigger writes to me what a Mr. Durgan is doing for the other nigger, and sends me a local paper, saying in effect how much better the Durgans are than the Courthopes. I acted on impulse—we Courthopes always do. It's the way of the world, you know—we should never do anything if it wasn't for trying to show that we are as good, or one better, than someone else. But if I'd known that folks here all lived on different mountains, I'd have let the Durgans have the field. Devilish cold at this altitude."

As he turned from the fire to speak he shivered, pushed up his collar still higher, and pulled his hat down almost to his eyes. He turned again to the fire. "Desperately cold up

here," he repeated.   "What's the name of this
mountain ?" he suddenly demanded.

They told him.

"'Deer Mountain.' I thought the driver said
'Bear Mountain.' I'm sure the nigger told me
to come up 'Bear.'"

"There is a peak of that name further off,"
said Alden.

"Ah well, I must say I am relieved to find
I've not come on a fool's errand, but have
achieved my purpose and discovered our friend,
Mr. Alden, although on another mountain. Odd
place this, where mountains have to be reckoned
like streets or squares. Well, Mr. Alden, my
business is just this : I'm willing to pay anything
in reason, and you can use bribery and cor-
ruption, or talent, or villainy, or anything else
you like as long as you get my man off. There
is my card ; and if you'll agree to undertake it,
I'd better drive back to the last village and try
to get a bed."

He did not take a step toward the door as he
spoke, but Durgan believed that he would fain
have done so.

Alden was standing very square, alert, and
upright. "Mr. Courthope, this is a very strange
thing. There is nothing that Adolphus knows

better than that I believe him to be guilty, and will not defend him."

The stranger expressed astonishment in word and action. He moved back a few steps, and sat down weakly on the bench by the wall; but Durgan observed that he thus neared the door, though appearing to settle himself for conversation.

"You are scarcely a hundred yards from the place where this 'Dolphus stabbed a beautiful quadroon woman, and left her dead," said Durgan. "She was found just here at——"

"How ghastly!" interrupted the other in unfeigned distress. "I confess to being afraid of ghosts—horribly afraid. But, gentlemen, I beg you to think what an awful business it would be to have that poor nigger hanged."

There was no doubt as to the truth of the emotion he now displayed, any more than in the matter of his former terror.

"It isn't fair, you know," he said; "for the punishment is out of all proportion to the crime, even if he is guilty. To be killed suddenly, when you are not expecting it, you know, is no suffering at all—nothing to compare with sitting for weeks expecting a horrible and deliberate end. Then the disgrace, the execration of the public." His thin voice had risen now in actual terror at the picture he had conjured up. "Save the poor devil if you can." His eyes turned instinctively toward Durgan's. " Sir, I do not know who you are, but I recognise a man of feeling and of honour. I protest the very thought of such a fate for this poor fellow appals me. I beseech you, have pity on the poor wretch, as you would desire pity in—in—your worst extremity."

He rose after he had spoken, moving about restlessly, as if in the attempt to control himself. His unfeigned appeal seemed to touch even Alden. His manner to the man suddenly became kinder."

" There is one thing that I can do for you," said the lawyer. " If you will write a short letter formally empowering me to find better counsel for the defence, I will—telegraph to a man I know in Atlanta to undertake it. Of course you must formally authorise me."

" Certainly ; certainly. I quite understand," said the stranger eagerly, coming toward the table where Alden was arranging paper.

" What's that ? " he said sharply, as he sat down.

There was a scrambling upon the hill above,

in which Durgan recognised the well-known run of Bertha with her dogs in leash. He determined at once to meet her and send her back, although he hardly knew why.

He said to Courthope evasively, "There are cattle grazing on all these hills."

At the moment he felt reproach for the lie, because the stranger seemed to trust him implicitly, for he seated himself and took the pen.

Alden surreptitiously kicked the damper of the small stove, increasing its heat, which was already great. He said to the stranger, who sat with his back to it, "You will catch cold in driving if you do not open your coat here."

Durgan left Alden to put the stranger through his paces, and went hastily round the ledge of the mine and swung himself up to the trail, meaning to intercept Bertha before she came near. He had not correctly estimated her pace, for when he emerged on the path she had just passed over it. He could only follow her as the girl descended by a light jump to the rock platform.

She was about forty feet from the door of the hut when she stood still and, turning, spoke : "My sister has a terrible attack of neuralgia. If the carriage is going back—we must send for the doctor. Who—who is it?"

In the next few confused moments Durgan was promising to send the message, seeking words to persuade her to return, and giving some answer to her question ; while Bertha was trying to hold the dogs still, and they, on the scent of strange footsteps, were straining on their leashes toward the door of the hut.

She was, perhaps, little loth to be pulled a few steps forward so that she could look in at the open door for herself. The lantern, which burned full in the face of the stranger, writing at the table, sent a long, bright stream outwards, in which Bertha now stood framed. In Durgan's memory afterwards this moment always remained with these two faces lit up at each end of the beam of light, while all around them was lost in darkness.

The stranger had thrown back his coat. His face was in clear profile.

Durgan himself was paralysed by the intensity of emotion which leaped to Bertha's face. She gave an inarticulate sound of terrified joy, a moan of heart-rending joy—or was it terror ?

The stranger, turning sharply, saw the girl, her face and figure illumined. His jaw dropped with terror. He stood up abjectly.

She sank to the ground, and Durgan, bending

U

over her, heard her trying to gasp a word with a wonderful intonation of tenderness and astonishment. That word was "Father." She tried again and again to speak it aloud.

She seemed fainting. Instinctively Durgan held the dogs, who broke into a howl of rage against the abject intruder.

As for the stranger, he appeared to become mad. Alden moved to the door to detain him, and was caught and thrown into the room as a child would be cast off by an athlete. The man had fled, and was lost in the gloom of the forest. He disappeared somewhere between the glow of the carriage lamps and Durgan's light, rushing down the hill.

Bertha had not wholly fainted. Now she was clinging to the collars of the dogs with her whole weight, grappling with them on the very floor of the rock. She was entreating Durgan in almost voiceless whispers to, "Go and bring him back. Go bring him."

Alden, who heard nothing Bertha said, was on the road shouting to the driver, "That man is mad. He is dangerous. Head him off down the road. Don't let him escape." The words rang sharp.

That portion of the hill into which the stranger had run was bordered by the rock precipice, which came up to the road beyond where the carriage stood.

Alden raised his voice to a reverberating shout, addressing the fugitive. "Come back. If you don't come back we will loose the dogs."

Durgan was trying to take the furious dogs from the girl, but she would not relax her hold. She was crying and moaning to the dogs to quiet them, and entreating Durgan to leave her with wild whispers. "Oh, save him; for God's sake, save him. Bring him back to me." She ground her teeth in anger at Alden's shout. "For pity's sake, stop that cruel man shouting. Call him off," she demanded, as if Alden were a dog; "call him off."

Durgan followed Alden. "She won't give you the dogs," he said.

"It was the sight of the dogs that frightened him," said Alden. "He is a maddened criminal, and a very dangerous man, whoever he may be. His weakness was feigned. He's skulking; but he's as good as caught, for he can't get over the precipice."

Durgan heard Bertha dragging and coaxing the dogs up the trail. In a few minutes she would have them shut up. He felt glad of this. In Alden's anger there was no mercy.

The driver was making torches with sticks, lamp oil, and a bit of rope. Before long, the three men had a glare which so illumined the wood that each tree-trunk threw a sharp, black shadow. They distributed the lights to lessen the shadows. They hunted all the slope between the road and the rock wall, but the fugitive was not found.

"If he had fallen over we should certainly have heard the fall," they said.

The silent driver added, "He swore he'd be good for forty dollars if I'd get him here and back; reckon I ain't the man to lose half a chance of that. I kep' my ears open; he ain't rolled over."

Book III

CHAPTER XXXI

THE bank shelved : no one could come on the precipice unwarned. Soon they found a travelling boot, and after that, at some distance, another. They felt sure now that the fugitive had climbed one of the trees, throwing away his boots as far as possible. Looking up, they perceived the hopelessness, in that case, of their quest. The arms of the forest spread out above them thick, gnarled, and black with the heaviest foliage of the year. The flame of their torches glared only on the under side of the boughs. Light and shadow were thrown in fantastic patches into the higher canopies, where also the lurid smoke of their torches curled.

They went back to the road ; the small, neat New Yorker tripping first, his torch dying, the boots of the fugitive in his other hand ; the driver, in old, loose coat, striding indolently toward the horses ; Durgan, lingering as he went, with sinewy arm throwing his light high and looking upward.

Alden examined the boots by the lamp in the hut. "These are New York boots," he said. Then he turned to the half-written letter on the table. "This writing I made him do is in a feigned hand." Alden's eyes were ablaze with angry excitement. "Look!" he cried. In the lining of the boots he had found a mark in ink. The initials were "J. C. B." "Can he be Beardsley, masquerading as a Southerner?"

"I begin to think he has done some years of masquerading as Beardsley."

"What do you mean?"

But Durgan went no further. His own uncertainty, Alden's obvious exhaustion, and the desire to let things sift themselves, kept him silent.

Something more alert than weary human sense was required for the vigil. Durgan went to the stable to get the terrier. He purposely took his way near the window of the sisters, anxious as to the nature of Bertha's excitement and her sister's illness.

But after passing the tranquil house, he found that Bertha had not entered it. She still stood outside the locked door of the stable in which she had chained the dogs. She leaned back against the door, looking up at the quiet light in her sister's window. Durgan lit a match, and held it in the pink lantern of his fingers until it was big enough to give them both a clear momentary view of each other. To his surprise, Bertha appeared to be in a quiet mood. The spark fell, and again only her light dress glimmered in the night. The first fine drops of gathering rain were falling.

He did not like a calm that seemed to him unnatural. He told her of the watch kept below, and of his errand.

She answered, "I am glad you have come. I don't know how to go to Hermie. Poor Hermie! How we have wronged her! But I am afraid to tell her, for it might kill her to-night. It was some cruel plan of Mr. Alden's, I know. I am afraid to go to her; but I am afraid, too, to leave her alone as ill as she is. She might die; though I don't think she will, because she always seems to have God with her; and, do you know, I have a queer feeling to-night that God may be here. It would seem better, of course, if we could all three die to-night; but in that case, why have we lived to meet again? No; there must be some way out, because Hermie has prayed so much—prayer must make some difference, don't you think?"

"I don't like to hear you talking in this mild, reasonable way. Are you not excited? Why do you not cry?"

"I was so dreadfully excited that I thought I was going mad; and then seemed to grow all still inside, as if there was no need to be afraid. I can't explain. The reason I'm talking is that I want you to tell me what to do. I've told you the danger of telling Hermie, and the danger of not going to her; and then, too, I want to go. down the hill. If I went alone, he would come to me and speak to me. He must be cold and hungry and tired. In the old days we never let a draught blow upon him. And he is so terribly thin, and has done something so dreadful with his hair, because I suppose he was afraid of being known. I ought to go to him."

"You must not stand here and go on talking like this. You must go at once into the house and nurse your sister. And you must not tell her what you are fancying or thinking about. If you do, it will make her very ill, and it will be your fault. You have wronged her terribly, as you say. Rouse yourself, and make some amends."

"Well—I will." She began to move with docility, but talked as he walked with her.

"Could you not send Mr. Alden down to the Cove on some pretence? And then, you know, we could find him, and I could bring him into the kitchen, at least, and give him warm wine —he used to like warm wine—and get him to bed without Hermie knowing. Dear Mr. Durgan, couldn't you do this for Hermie's sake? You know it is what she would like."

Durgan took her by the arm. "Miss Bertha, you have, perhaps, made a mistake. It is very easy to make such mistakes under excitement such as you have passed through to-night. That excitement has almost killed your sister, and it has probably made you fanciful."

"Yes—but then, how was it *he* knew *me*?"

"He saw the dogs. He may have supposed they were brought to seize him, and so he bolted."

She replied in the same voice as before. "But then, this explains Hermie's secret. What else could? You know we said nothing could, but this does."

Durgan felt that, perhaps, her mind had become a blank, and her voice was answering with his own thoughts, which within him were holding the same dialogue.

"What are you saying?" he said roughly.

"How can your father be alive? And if he were, do you understand that he must have killed the other man?"

He had struck the right note. She pulled herself from him with natural recoil. "Yes, yes; and that is clear from Hermie's action, too. But you don't know what happened. There must be some excuse."

"You know, Miss Bertha, you have thought very foolish things before; you may not be right now."

She sat down on the edge of the verandah, and began to weep heartily and quietly. He was relieved: tears proved her well-being.

They had come, walking together, to that end of the house where, on the second day of their acquaintance, he had found her at dawn watching over his safety. He looked about now, and longed for the dawn, but there was nothing but glimmering darkness and the sweet smell of the gathering rain.

When Bertha had cried for a while she went in to her sister. In a minute she came tip-toeing back to Durgan.

"Hermie is sleeping quite restfully," she said. "How much softer the air feels; I think the change has done her good."

As he turned away Durgan's heart sank. The belief that Claxton was the murderer, not the murdered, and had been sheltered all these years by his own wife, forced itself upon Durgan. These innocent women might find rest in the softened air ; but what rest could that woman who bore his name ever find, whose cruelty and selfishness must, in consequence of the exposure now imminent, bear the light of public shame ?

CHAPTER XXXII

DURGAN took the terrier and led him up and down through the bit of sequestered woodland; but the animal, beyond enjoying the unusual festivity of a night walk, exhibited no sense of the situation. It stopped to bark at no tree foot, and although it resented the intrusion of the driver, discovered nothing else to resent.

The slow-tongued driver made another remark. "That's a queer thing, too. I'd have thought he'd have barked at a cat in a tree, I would."

Durgan had despised Alden in the vicious snap of his pitiless anger against the fugitive; but as the night wore on, and he saw his face grow more and more haggard, as if he were aged by a decade since the last sun shone, he was glad to procure him rest or relief of any sort.

Confident that the dog would give warning if the prisoner climbed down, Alden accepted the use of Durgan's bed ; but it was easy to see that he could not rest. There was the constant secret movement of one who was pretending to be still.

"Perhaps you would rather talk," said Durgan. "I wish you would tell me all you know about Miss Claxton's father. Is she like him ?"

"Not at all. I found little to respect in his character."

"I suppose you dug up his past very thoroughly."

"There was nothing in it but selfishness and vanity. He was of old colonial stock, but had been ill-reared to leisure and luxury—the worst training in a new country, where these things involve no corresponding responsibilities. He married into a plain New England family for the sake of money. The mother of Hermione, I need not say, was immensely his superior ; but she died at the birth of the second daughter. There is some disparity of age between them— Hermione——"

Durgan had to bring him back from reminiscences of his love.

"Ah—as to Claxton's ill health, if it interests you, I judge that it dated from a blow to his vanity. He was very worldly, and, when a widower, did a good deal of amateur acting, and became engaged to marry a young beauty who had just come out as a public singer. Society took her up. She was the belle of the season, and jilted Claxton. It was a matter of talk; but I don't suppose his daughters ever heard of it—daughters don't hear such things, you know. He kept them in a country boarding-school, where, I am happy to say, Hermione got religion."

Durgan smiled to himself over the quaint phrase used so seriously. "But the father?"

"He married in pique a dull pink and white society woman, with more money; and then became a chronic invalid. When he was tired of his wife he sent for his daughters. I never heard that he was unkind to them, or to his wife; but it seemed to me he only cared for them as they devoted themselves to his comfort. Hermione—often has she discussed it with me—was very anxious as to his spiritual state. It was her great desire that he should seek salvation. It was that desire that caused her always such distress when her father finally dabbled in spiritualism. His death, in a still ungodly state, was, I can aver, her worst trouble in all that terrible chain of events. She felt so much that she never mentioned her concern about him again."

Alden had been speaking in a sleepy way, as if his recent distrust of his chosen lady was obliterated by some fragrance from the poppy beds of weariness and love and night.

He slept at last. The bleakness of the mountain night had given place to a balmy rain.

Durgan pondered. He knew that his wife would bow down to one like Claxton, who had had the social ball at his feet; she would regard his intimate knowledge of the society she desired to cajole as a most valuable property, and would risk much to retain it.

When the grey morning came they went out to the trees again, but no one was hiding among them.

Then they went down by the road, and climbed along to the foot of the precipice; but, making the closest search along its base, they found nothing.

Alden became racked by a new fear: the unknown had perhaps cheated them, and recrossed the road. The desperate condition of the man, the women unprotected—these thoughts were so terrible that he ran up the hill to protect them, unconscious that his valour was out of all proportion to his frame.

x

When he was gone the driver said, "Forty dollars didn't get the better of me crossin' that road while I kep' an eye on it, I reckon."

The mountain forest dripped and trickled, the dry ground soaking in the moisture with almost audible expansion of each atom of earth, each pore of fern and leaf, and the swelling of twigs. The wet and glisten everywhere deepened the colour of rock and wood, moss, lichen, and weed.

The driver stood considering the face of the rock; the terrier began nosing among some fallen leaves; Durgan was looking this way and that, to see which might have invited the nearest temporary hiding. Alden had believed the stranger's weakness a pretence; Durgan believed the strength he had shown to be the transient effect of fear.

The driver at length said, "Hi! Look here. What's that?"

He pointed to a black bundle in a fissure of the precipice.

"That there fur coat! I'll be blowed! He got down here, sir; and he had the devil to help him—leastwise, reckoning from all I have seen this night, I conclude that Satan was in the concern. He climbed down that crack in the rock, sir, and caught on by the bushes on the way, and scrambled along that slantwise bit, and then he got hold of the tree. He warn't killed or maimed or he'd be here."

"Then we've lost him."

"Mr. Bantam Cock will perhaps be sending despatches for to apprehend him at the different steam-car depôts, for to get my forty dollars."

"Say we make it fifty ?"

"Well, sir ; I would say, 'thank you.'"

"And that would be all you would say, mind you, or I'll have you turned off at the hotel."

"Then I won't even say that, sir. There ain't anything comes easier to me than shuttin' up, I reckon."

After this colloquy, which passed quickly, Durgan was turning upwards when he heard a horse ascending the road. In a few minutes he had met his two negro labourers coming to their work, and, behind them, the doctor from Hilyard, riding, as he usually did, with saddle-bags, his old buff clothes much bespattered.

"The yellow nigger is dead, Mr. Durgan. He died last night with the change of the weather. You told me to keep him alive till you came, but you didn't come. He was a very curious fellow—not half bad ; and his last freak was to ask me to come and tell you to look sharp after the visitor he sent you.   So, as you're not much out of my way to-day, I've come at once."

He got off his horse, and the two men talked together.

The doctor, whose ordinary round comprised anything within a radius of thirty miles, had not been in Hilyard when the rich traveller from New Orleans arrived and started again.   His wealth and imperious airs had impressed the little town, but beyond the fact that he had gained a private interview with the dying prisoner, nothing was known about him.

"And the odd thing is," said the doctor, "that 'Dolphus sent the jailer with every cent he had in the world—about fifteen dollars—to bribe the driver.   As to his health, he was decidedly better, and when this Mr. Courthope turned up he seems to have acted like a well man, and made him believe he was well.   When I got home there was a report about that the stranger was a wonder-worker, and had cured him.   But when I went to him the fever was up.   After his last flash in the pan he burnt out in a few hours."

Durgan supposed there might be something of greater importance to justify the doctor's ride.

"Perhaps," he said, "he asked you to bring a message to Mr. Alden or Miss Smith?"

"He was a most extraordinary fellow," said the other. "I never was quite sure when he was talking sense and when nonsense. But the message was to you; and it was that you were to keep this Courthope, and write to the chief of police in New York and claim the reward offered in the Claxton case. And you are to give as much of the money to Adam as you think will pay for his wife. He said he'd die easy if I'd give you that tip; and he did die easy."

Durgan smiled sadly at the pathos of the dying nigger's interest in his fellows and his desire for justice to be done. "Did you reckon him wandering?"

"That's just as you choose to take it," said the doctor. "I'm accustomed to hearing secrets and forgetting them. My only business before I forget this one is to ascertain that a dangerous character is not left at large. If you cannot give me that assurance, I suppose I ought to tell the police myself."

Durgan felt that the case of the Claxton sisters had now reached extremity, and, much against his will, he replied in a nonchalant tone, "We must come and talk the matter over with Mr.

Alden." He saw no means of securing the runaway or of hiding the scandal—he hardly desired to hide it. He felt stunned at the shame that must fall on his wife.

As they turned the doctor said, "You think this yellow fellow and his sort mere trash, Mr. Durgan; but I'm inclined to think he would have made a good citizen with any sort of training. He had more public spirit than ten of our corrupt politicians rolled into one."

"Perhaps so," said Durgan absently. "I may be prejudiced."

He whistled the dog, and heard nothing at first, but then, from a nook below the hill, came an answering yelp. The yelp was repeated.

The driver, who had been standing passive at a distance, sauntered nearer. "There's something queer about that dog. He's been down there a powerful while. If he'd found another shoe he'd bark like that. And mebbe there's another shoe still to find, sir, for if two fits out a man, a man in conjunction with the devil might require two more."

Durgan took the hint, and went down towards the dog. He was puzzled by its peculiar call. It came a little way to meet him, crawling and fawning, but returned swiftly whither it came.

In a few minutes more Durgan was looking down on the prostrate body of the unknown traveller. He was lying straight and flat on his back; his eyes were open, and they met Durgan's with a mournful look of full intelligence which, in that position, was more startling than the glazed eye of death. The terrier licked the hand that lay nearest the face, then licked the brow very gently just for a moment, and yelped again.

"Why don't you get up?"

The stranger's lips moved. Durgan had to kneel to hear the thick effort at speech.

"Paralysed!"

The lips moved feebly to let Durgan know that, after his escape, the seizure had come as he fled. The doctor came, and gently moved hand and foot, testing the muscles and nerves. He confirmed the self-diagnosis. The stricken man had probably lain unconscious half through the night, but his mind was clear now.

The rain had washed the temporary dye and all the stiffness from his hair. It lay grey and dishevelled about his thin, brown face. The haggard lines were partly gone; the dark eyes looked up steadily, sad as eyes could be, but fearless.

The change was so great that Durgan spoke

his involuntary sympathy. "Guess you feel nothing worse can come to you now." Then he added, "Keep up your heart. I'll take you where you will be well cared for."

The driver had followed slowly, and looked on without query.

"You bet," he said at length ; "the devil's gone out of him."

Durgan wondered if that was actually what had happened when Bertha felt the peace of God, and Hermione slept, and the wretched mulatto found ease in death.

"He had over exerted," said the doctor, "and all the tonic went out of the air when the rain fell."

CHAPTER XXXIII

THEY went back to Durgan's hut, and made a stretcher of his bed, and brought down his labourers as carriers.

A curious group walked slowly up the zigzag road to the summit house : Durgan and the terrier walked one on each side ; the doctor rode behind. There was naught to be said ; they walked in silence. Sometimes the eyelids of the still face drooped ; again they were opened wide. The wet forest breathed about their silence the whisper of the rain.

When the party came in sight of the house gable, someone who was sitting in the window of the sisters' room seemed to see them and moved away. The place was astir for the day. Smoke was rising from the chimneys, and the soft-voiced coloured servant was singing to a Southern melody one of the doggerel hymns of her race :—

"De Lord He sent His angel.
   (Fly low, sweet angel ;
   Fly low, sweet angel ;
   Comin' for deliver us again.)
  An' He tamed de lions for Daniel ;
  An' for Peter broke de prison and de chain.
   O ! de angel of de Lord."

The servant was at work in an outer kitchen ; the very words were clear. The gentle melody of the stanza was ended abruptly by the soft, triumphal shout of the last line.

Durgan made the labourers rest their burden within the doorway of the barn, while he went forward with the doctor. But now from the back door Hermione came. She was clad in the simple grey morning gown which she always wore at her housewife's duties ; but she looked a shadow of herself, so pale and wan with the pain of the night. She came forward quickly. Durgan saw at a glance that she knew what Bertha could tell, and was ready to meet whatever evil was sufficient for the day. Even at such a moment, so selfless and courteous was she, she had a modest word of greeting and gratitude for Durgan.

Durgan made the doctor tell her the truth quickly, and Hermione went straight on to the side of the nerveless man.

Almost as soon as she looked, without a moment's betrayal of unusual emotion, she stooped and kissed him.

In thick utterance the paralytic repeated her name. What he thought or felt none might know ; the still features gave no expression.

Then a great joy lit up her face, and the tone of her homely words was like a song of praise.

"We can keep you safe. You will be quite safe here ; and Birdie and I will take real good care of you. We have a beautiful home ready for you."

The doctor had turned away. She gave her command to the bearers, and walked with new lightness beside the bed as it was carried toward the house.

Durgan followed, and found that he was holding his hat in his hand.

How terrible, indeed, was this meeting of love and lack-love, of the life gained by self-giving and the life lost by self-saving. The woman, at one with all the powers of life—body, mind, and spirit a unity—able (rare self-possession) to give herself when and for whom she would ; meeting with this self-wrecked, disintegrated man, for whom she had suffered and was still eager to suffer. Like most things of divine import, that kiss given by the very principle of life to the soul lying in moral death had passed without observation.   Durgan looked upon the still face. He could now clearly recognise the likeness to Bertha in the form, colour, and inward glow of the eyes ; but so fixed and expressionless were the muscles of the face, which had taken on a look of sensuous contentment, that the onlooker could not even guess what that glow of suffering might betoken, how much there was of memory, of shame, of remorse, of any love for aught but self, or how much latent force of moral recuperation there might be.

While they went on to the house through the tears of the morning, the negress with the velvet voice was still singing.

> " An' de Lord He sent His angel,
> An' He walked wi' de children in de flame.
> (Fly low, sweet angel.) "

Durgan, who had been feeling like one in a dream, suddenly forgot to listen to the song, for he saw, as in a flash, the cause of Hermione's solemn joy.   The criminal had been restored to her in the only way in which it was possible for his life to be preserved for a time, and for him to be allowed to die in peace.   Neither Alden, nor any other, could propose to bring this stricken man to answer in an earthly court. It was again her privilege to lavish love upon him, to reap the result of her sacrifice by tending his lingering life and telling him her treasure of faith—of the mercy of God and the hope of heaven.

CHAPTER XXXIV

DURGAN felt that day to be a distinctly happy one. A youth makes many pictures of happiness for himself, and he must have but a poor outfit of hope and imagery whose pictures are realised. Yet happiness springs up beside the steps of the older wayfarer, a wild flower that he has not sown or tended. In places where his familiar burden lightens, or when gathering clouds disperse, it pushes up its bright flower-face with a positive beauty and fragrance, something much fairer and better than the mere negation of trouble, yet not so gay as mere imagined joys. Durgan, who had come to this mountain thinking to be alone, and had become so strenuously involved in the fate of his neighbours, to-day not only felt peace in the cessation of fear and gloomy forebodings which had enwrapped them all, but was lifted beyond this to participate in the joy of heavenly deliverance which transfigured Hermione Claxton. He could not think of her to-day without a strange, new, selfless pleasure which he did not analyse; and, added to this, his heart leaped up in gratitude on his own account, for surely now the wife he was bound to honour would be spared the public odium which to her vain nature would be peculiar agony. The fate of a long, living death for the man who had stifled every honourable impulse to avoid the legal punishment of death was robbed of its worst horror, because it gave him immunity from the passion of fear by which he was enslaved, and restored him to the arms of the only human love which could not be quenched by his misconduct and disgrace. Durgan knew enough to suppose that when his wife's first glamour of reverence for Claxton had passed, when, with the help of such a skilful prompter, she had succeeded on the stage of her ambition, his home with her had been no longer even peaceful. The letters 'Dolphus had stolen had convinced Durgan that she was prepared to get rid of her protégé if possible; and when he left her he was practically a homeless fugitive, the whole world his enemy. From such a fate self-destruction, or yielding to the last penalty of the law, were the only ways of escape, had not the angel of mercy intervened.

Later in the day Alden came from the room above the carriage-house, the room in which Durgan had spent his first two curious nights on Deer Mountain. He only knew of the finding of the fugitive, for, on being assured of this, he had fallen asleep in sheer exhaustion.

The rain was shifting for the time, affording intervals of blithe air and mellow sunlight. Alden sat him down upon a settle in the verandah. The trailing vines and the passion-flower were glowing with the life-renewing moisture, but the gorgeous leaves and long tassels of the love-lies-bleeding had fallen, sodden with the rain.

Durgan was waiting for some instructions concerning certain invalid requisites. His cousins, the Durgan Blounts, were returning to Baltimore for the winter, and Durgan had undertaken that they should make the purchases. No sooner had Alden spoken than Miss Claxton left her writing-desk, came swiftly, and sat down beside him.

"There is something that I am waiting to tell you," she said. Her voice was very gentle. "I have not made any explanation, either, to Mr. Durgan, for I wouldn't till I saw you ; but he ought to know, for Mrs. Durgan's sake."

Durgan had moved, but, at her command, remained.

There was a little silence, and after she began he was quite sure she had forgotten his presence. She took Alden's passive hand in hers.

"Herbert! my father has come back to us. No, dear; do not start like that. He is still alive. That is my long secret, which I could not have kept from you for anyone's sake but his."

Alden said not a word. He sat erect, as if someone had struck him.

"Oh," she cried, with tears in her voice, "the fate that came to him that terrible morning was worse than death, and now he has been carried back to us paralysed. Have patience with me, and I will tell you all that happened."

The little lawyer, as if suddenly moved by some electric force, was for bounding from his seat, every nerve quivering with the sting of his own mortification and the shock of surprise. It was the strength of her will that controlled him.

"I must tell you from the beginning—it is the only way. Upon the morning that that crime was committed in our house, a boy came with a note from Mr. Beardsley. It made my father very angry. He told me that Beardsley was coming on the heels of his messenger upon an impertinent errand. What he said was that

Y

Beardsley was bent upon dictating the terms of his friendship with Mrs. Durgan, whom he had only lately met.

"There was something the maids had to do that afternoon, and I sent them then in the morning, for I could not bear that anyone should see such a person in our house, or see my father so angry. My poor step-mother had not risen from bed. When Beardsley came he went up-stairs to my father's sitting-room. The door was shut, but from what my father told me after-wards, I know pretty well what happened."

"Afterwards," repeated Alden; "afterwards I Hermione ?"

"Dear Herbert, do not be angry, but only listen, and you will understand how easily what seemed impossible could happen. This Mr. Beardsley had the idea that my poor father and Mrs. Durgan had fallen in love at his meetings. He was a simple, stupid man, and he thought it his duty to exhort my father and warn my step-mother. I think that, angry as he was, my father thought it best to receive his exhortation with the affectation of playfulness. It was his way, you know. He had graceful, whimsical ways; he was not like other people. When he could not make this man see his own folly, or divert him from his purpose, he took down the little old pistol that was fastened on the wall as an ornament—the one that was found. I need not tell you that he did not know it was loaded ; I did not know, and I dusted his things every day, for he could not bear to have a servant in the room. He tried to stop Beardsley by threatening to shoot himself in mock despair. Poor mamma, hearing loud voices, ran in.

"Up till then I am sure papa had not a serious thought, except that he was naturally angered by the folly of the man ; but the pistol went off, and poor mamma was killed. Oh ! can you not imagine my father's wild grief and anger against the fellow that, as he would think, had caused him to do it ? But there was more than that. My father told me that Beardsley denounced him as a wilful murderer, and declared that it was only a feigned accident. Then, you see, he was the only witness, and could ruin my father's reputation. Oh, I think it was fear as much as anger, but I am sure it was frenzy, possessed my father. You know what happened. The Indian battle-axe was hanging beside the pistol, and as soon as Beardsley fell, I am sure my father lost all control of himself or any knowledge of what he was doing."

"Hermione," said Alden, "you cannot believe this story? Who has made you believe it?" He lifted her hand to his lips. "Have you believed this all these years?"

"It is true, Herbert; you will have to believe it. I will tell you my part in it. I do not think I did right, but you will see that I did not know what else to do. When I heard the noise I ran upstairs, but the door was locked. The boy that brought the note was waiting in the kitchen all this time for Beardsley to pay him. Then, in a minute, all was quiet, and I heard my father sobbing like a child. You cannot think how quickly it all happened. Then my father came to the door, and whispered through, 'Hermione, are you alone? Are the servants out? Is Bertha there?' So I told him of Beardsley's messenger waiting below.

"Then he came out and called over the stairs to the boy. You know how very clever and quick he always was when he wanted to do anything. He looked the boy up and down, and then he said, 'Do you want to earn a hundred dollars?' The boy was cautious; he did not answer. My father said, 'Can you hold your tongue and help me, and I'll make a gentleman of you? It's your best chance, for a crime has been committed in this house, and if you don't do as I bid you, I'll give you up to the police and say you did it ; they'll take my word for it.' And all the time, between speaking, he was sobbing. He shoved the boy into his dressing-room. Then he told me what had happened.

" He told me he would be hanged if I did not keep quite quiet. I could not believe that they were dead. I went into the room, but I couldn't stop an instant. The sight of that poor body, disfigured past all recognition, even the clothes stained beyond recognition, made me almost insensible. I saw that no doctor could be of any use.

" My father was very quick. He shaved himself, and coloured his face with his paints, and put on the boy's clothes. He told me he would go to Mrs. Durgan, who would get him away. He told me to call the police at once, and tell them everything except that I had seen him or knew anything about him. He locked the boy in a narrow cupboard that held hot-water pipes, and told me how to let him out at night. I did not think at the time it could be wrong to keep silence about my father. I did just what he told me to do.

" You know, Herbert, you said the other

night that I had deceived you ; but, indeed, the
great deceit came of itself. I don't think even
my father intended it. I could never have believed they could have mistaken that man lying
there for my father. First, the police made the
mistake ; then, in a few hours, we heard the
newsboys crying it all over the streets. Still I
felt sure that when you came, and the coroner,
the truth would be known. When you believed
it, too, what word could I have said to you that
would not have made it your duty to hunt him
down ? His daughter was the only person who
could take the responsibility of silence. I don't
say I was right to do it ; I only know I could
not do anything else. Even the boy, as I found
afterwards, had never seen Beardsley. A servant
had given him the note to bring. He naturally
thought it was Beardsley who had bribed him
and escaped in his clothes. I only kept silent
hour by hour.

"I thought again they would find out at the
inquest ; but when, at length, the poor body
was buried, and those saturated, torn clothes
burned, and I had found out from Mrs. Durgan
that the poor wretch had no near relatives or
friends to mourn him, I could no nothing but
acquiesce. I had a message from father, through

Mrs. Durgan, before they arrested me. She and he had decided that he must personate the dead man, and he even ventured to play the medium's part at the dark séance. He was always clever at disguises. I could not judge them. I hardly cared, then, whether I lived or died ; the wickedness of it all was so dreadful. I shrank far more—and there was nothing heroic in that—from the thought of my father being arrested and punished than from danger for myself. Think what it would have been like if it had been your father ! "

Seeing that Alden was profoundly distressed, she hastened to say, " If I had told you, Herbert, how painful would your position have been ! And I never even told Bertha ; it was father's parting request that she should not know. But I know that of late she has guessed something, for she has lived in fear up here alone. I was obliged when I was ill in Paris to tell her where she would find the truth ; she guessed the rest, I fear, and it must have been father's return that she has dreaded. But now he has been brought back so helpless he can never hurt anyone again."

Alden's emotion was hardly restrained from breaking through the crust of his conventionality, and Hermione was fain to turn to a lighter aspect of the case in addressing Durgan.

"I gathered from my father's letters that Mrs. Durgan's motive in befriending him was partly kindness, and partly that he could be of use to her."

"I can understand that," said Durgan. He also felt it a relief to speak clearly on the only aspect of this sorrowful tale which did not awaken emotion. "It was the one thing in the whole world that my wife wanted—to be told how to manipulate the secret springs of a world of fashion in which she had so far moved as one in the dark. And having once taken your father in, she could not go back."

He rose as she said this and went away, wondering much how Alden would submit to the continued devotion of such a daughter to such a father, how much Hermione's appeal would reach him : "Think how you would feel if it were your father."

CHAPTER XXXV

A DAY or two later Alden was returning to New York. Durgan drove him to Hilyard in Miss Claxton's surrey.

All the mountains had begun to wear golden caps. Lower down the yellow pod of the wild pea and purple clusters of wild grapes were tangled in the roadside bushes. The sun shone, and the birds cawed and chirped as they quarrelled for the scarlet berries of the ash ; not a bird sang, for it was not nesting-time.

"The doctor can't make a guess, then, as to how long Claxton may live ? It may be for months, I suppose," said Durgan.

Alden drew himself up in the attitude of one who gives an important opinion. He was going back to his world of conventions, and already taking on its ways. "My dear sir, I see no reason why, with such nursing, surrounded by such luxuries, in the finest air, and in such tranquillity, he should not live—ah, perhaps for years."

"It will not be so long as that, I think."

"That must be as God wills."

But there was too much religious starch in the tone of these words to suggest acquiescence.

This good little man, with all his constancy and fervour, had not a large enough soul to see so vile a prodigal feasted without resentment.

Said Durgan, "If his mind is as lucid as the doctor thinks, his present experience must be pretty much like lying helpless in a lake of fire."

"Sir, what is there to trouble him ? Two of the finest, most agreeable women who ever lived on this earth, are his slaves. They wheel him hither and thither as he suggests a preference. They read ; they sing ; they show him nature in her glory ; and his body suffers no pain. I do not understand your allusion."

"I thought it just possible that, being human, he might have a soul latent in him."

"'Soul' ! He has, without excuse or provocation, committed the most brutal crime of the decade ; he has passed his years since ministering to his own tastes and indolences in the society of a lady who pleased his fancy, while, with the most horrid cruelty and worm-like cowardice, he has left his tender daughter to suffer the consequences of his crime. He has within him, sir, a soul, humanly speaking, beyond hope of redemption."

"But Christian faith compels his daughter to set aside the human aspects of the case."

"Women, sir—women have no standard of manly virtue. Can you conceive that a son—a man who knew the world, could slur over such vice, such perfidy, in a parent?"

Alden's reiteration of "Sir," spoken between his teeth, had so very much the force of "Damn you," that Durgan forbore to suggest that the point of his remark had been evaded.

Alden, half conscious of his own angry inconsistency as a religious man in desiring the torment of the wicked, still resented Durgan's logic enough to bring forward at this point an unpalatable subject. "With regard to Mrs. Durgan, sir ; from all the inquiries I have made, I understand that she probably was aware that Adolphus, who has been his valet all these years, had summoned Claxton here on threat of disclosure, and that Claxton had gone to New Orleans, there to assume this new incognito—which, knowing the negro's origin, was natural enough before he interfered on his behalf in your neighbourhood. But I understand that Mrs. Durgan did not know that I or the ladies were here, and had no suspicion of the servant's intended treachery. In all probability she has not heard from Claxton, at any rate since he left New Orleans. You are aware that we have decided that the Miss Claxtons shall, till their father's death, retain the name they took upon entering this neighbourhood. I wish to suggest to you that it would not be safe to trust Mrs. Durgan with the secret of their whereabouts. It is undesirable, in keeping a secret, to trust human nature any further than is absolutely necessary, and it appears to me, therefore, needful to request you to let Mrs. Durgan be left in entire ignorance of the fate of her late protégé."

Durgan could not but inwardly admit that there was a certain poetic justice in leaving his wife thus in a condition of suspense, and although he resented the manner of the instruction, he expressed conditional acquiescence.

Durgan more than suspected that Alden was querulously wreaking upon the criminal, and upon all he met, the anger he felt against himself for not, at the first, discerning the simple mistake which had caused the mystery of the " Claxton case." As they drove on, mile after mile, through the wild harvests of the woodland, this supposition was confirmed. After talking of many things, Alden broke out in self-soothing comment—

"As to the mistake of the murdered man's identity, my dear sir, how could doubt enter the mind? The body lay in Claxton's private room, beside the couch which he constantly occupied—an unrecognisable mass; Mrs. Claxton dead beside him, and neither of self-inflicted wounds; Bertha wailing the loss of her father; Hermione stunned by a shock of grief. Who the dead was, seemed so self-evident; who the murderer could be, such a puzzle, that the mind inevitably dwelt exclusively on the latter point. My dear sir, looking back on the matter, even now I cannot see how a suspicion of the truth could have arisen."

With his professional pique adding to his intense private grief for Hermione's long sacrifice, it was, perhaps, not surprising that the return of perfect confidence in her, after the agony of reluctant distrust, did not do more to sweeten the ferment of his little soul. Durgan reflected that on a mind no longer young, filled with long earlier memories of mutual trust, the suspicion of a few recent days could make little impression. And, again, this short-lived emotion of suspicion was succeeded by the pain of knowing that his own happiness and hers had been voluntarily sacrificed for a wretch so devoid of any trace of chivalry or of parental feeling.

Before reaching Hilyard, Alden expressed his opinion upon another aspect of the recent disclosure. "You say, sir, that to you the most amazing part is that such a man as Claxton could do so deadly a deed. My dear sir, my experience of crime is that the purely selfish nature only needs the spark of temptation to flame out into some hellish deed. No doubt you will think me puritanical, but I hold that, while to most cultured egoists such temptation never comes, in God's sight they are none the less evil for that mere absence of temptation. Idleness and self-love, especially where education enhances the guilt, are the dirt in which the most virulent plague-germs can propagate with speed and fecundity."

Durgan felt that, whether this opinion was true or false, it was brought forward now with an energy directed against the class to which he himself belonged.

The two men parted stiffly, but they both felt that Alden would return in a more placable mood.

That day, in a burying-ground near Hilyard,

the mulatto called "'Dolphus" was laid beneath the ground.   Born the ward of a nation whose institutions had first brought about his existence and then severed him from his natural protectors, he had been given only a little knowledge by way of life's equipment, which, murderer as he was, had proved in his hands a less dangerous thing than in those of many a citizen of the dominant race.   No one in that great nation mourned his death or gave a passing sigh to his lone burial ; and if anyone set store by that bare patch of grave cut in the unkempt grass among the wild field lilies it must have been God, who is said to gather what mortals cast away.

Durgan took Adam back to Deer with him. Adam was somewhat the worse for the success of his grief and piety, genuine though they were. These qualities had won him praise and consideration ; they were no longer unconscious. Like a child who had been on a stage, he was inclined to pose and show elaborate signs of grief.

Durgan bore with him for a few days and then spoke his mind.

"Stop that, you absurd nigger !   If you don't look alive I'll make you !"

Adam paused in the middle of a pious ejaculation with his mouth open.

"Reckon you don't know what I'll do to you."

"No, Marse Neil. How can this pore child know your mind, suh?"

"I'll have you married to the new girl Miss Smith got. I'll do it next week!"

Adam rolled his eyes heavenward. "An' the Lord only just took my pore gal, suh! You's not in earnest, suh?"

"And if I make you marry the new girl the Lord will have given you a better one."

Adam was deftly cooking Durgan's breakfast, moving about the hut with the light step of pride in the new service.

There was a silence. Durgan had become absorbed in the newspaper.

At last, with another sigh that was cut short ere it had expanded his huge chest, Adam meekly began—

"Marse Neil, suh."

"Well?"

"The minister who visited me in my affliction, he say—sez he—that we ought to take wi' joy all the dealing of the Lord an' bless His name."

And Durgan replied, without raising his eyes, "I believe it. Adam, you are a good nigger. I'll speak to Miss Smith."

One day, a while after, the young gardener against whose aspirations Durgan had warned Bertha came up to the mica mine. He had left Deer Cove soon after Bertha had dismissed him, and gone, as the old stories have it, "into the world to seek his fortune." It was a very unusual step for a mountain white, and had given his father so much concern that he had had the son prayed for at the Sunday camp meeting. The errant gardener had roamed as far as Baltimore, and worked a while in the household of a certain rich man. He had come away from the plutocrat's palace homesick for his mountains, but had brought back one dominant idea. Probably his disappointed love had made his mind peculiarly impressionable, or, true to the traditions of his class, he might, perhaps, not have gained even one. He had now the most exaggerated idea of the elevation to which the "rich and great" were raised. Convinced when he left Deer that Bertha would not receive his addresses, he had found consolation in investing her with a new glamour, as one of an almost princely cast. Upon his return he had heard the talk of the neighbourhood—the story which Alden had allowed to go abroad—that the invalid father, who had been leading some kind of dis-

z

sipated life abroad, had returned, after years of
estrangement, to be nursed in his last illness by
his daughters.   Herein lay the motive of young
Godson's errand.

"They say that he doesn't like coloured men
lifting him and moving him about—that Miss
Smith's looking for a helper for him."

Durgan laid his pick against the rock and
stood in silent astonishment.   He had seen
different emotions work different changes in the
habits of men, but never so remarkable a result
of love as this cure of petty pride in the stiff-
necked mountaineer.   He was uncertain how far
the young man had interpreted himself aright.

"It is for Miss Bertha's sake you wish to do
this ?" he asked.

Godson assented.

And having at last satisfied himself, by more
interrogation, that the youth had actually no
further hope at present than to serve his goddess
in some lowly task, Durgan undertook to support his application.

With this end in view he went up to the
summit house at his usual hour, when the day's
work was over, at sundown.

On the lawn the invalid's flat carriage was
tilted at an angle which enabled him to see the

delectable mountains bathed in the light reflected from that other country—the cloud-land beyond the golden river of the horizon, in which the sun, like a pilgrim, was going down. The elder daughter was reading to him.

Durgan had no mind to disturb them. He had come hoping that the paralytic would have been put away for the night. He disliked encountering Claxton ; and, had he disliked the man less, the wrestling soul that shone through the eyes of the almost inanimate face would have distressed him.

Bertha, who was sitting at a short distance from the pair, and out of their sight, saw the visitor and came across the grass.

They went for a stroll together up on the higher rocks.

"I am very idle in these days," said Bertha. "All the children in my nursery have grown up and are too big to be nursed. There is nothing to do even in the garden."

"But the care of your father must absorb all your time and thought."

As he said this there was a questioning inflection in his mind that he kept out of his tone.

She hung her head as she walked. After a while she spoke, a beautiful flush on her face.

"In the old days father loved me better than Hermie, because I was better looking, and I always thought all that he did was perfect. I thought I loved him far more than Hermie did, because she often tried to persuade him that what he did was wrong. Now——"

Durgan waited.

"Now he does not want to see me. He does not like me to talk or read to him. It makes it hard for Hermie, for she has everything to do. She thinks father is shy of me and that it will wear away."

"I have no doubt it will."

"No," she sighed; "you are both wrong. Father, in spite of his helplessness, sees far more clearly. He was always quick to read everyone. He knows "—her voice faltered—" that I cannot love him now that I know what he did. Oh, I hate him for deserting Hermie and letting her bear it!" She pressed her hand to her side, as if speaking of some disease that gave her pain. "How can I help it, Mr. Durgan? I despise him, and he knows it."

"I dare say he does. He knows, of course, that the whole world could regard him with no feelings but those of hatred and scorn."

She stopped short in her walk. In a minute

she said, "I think I will go back again, Mr. Durgan. I cannot bear that you should speak that way to me about my own father."

He smiled. "You seem to have some filial affection left."

"Did you only say it to make me feel angry?"

"Yes; that was why I said it; but, at the same time, you must remember that the world would certainly judge as you have said; and if the ties of kindred did not give a closer embrace than the world does, there would be no home feeling for any of us; there would be no bright spark of the sacred fire of the next world in this."

"'Fire.' We think of heaven as light, not heat."

"And we think of hell as heat, not light: yet we know light and heat to be one and the same thing; and both are the supreme need of life, and both are the only adequate symbols of love."

Many a red flag and gay pennon of autumn was now flying on the heights of Deer. The leaves of the stunted oak wood were floating and falling, and below, the chestnuts were yellowing, burr and leaf. The weeds were sere and full of ripe seed, and the shrubs of ripe berries. Birds of passage in flocks were talking and calling, eating their evening meal, or settling, a noisy multitude, in verdant lodging for the night.

" I always wonder where they have come from, or where they are going," said the girl. " I used to long so often, in all the nights and days I have been on this mountain, to be able to fly away as the birds fly ; and now, since Eve died, what we have suffered makes me feel that just to live here, away from the worse sorrows of the world, would be enough happiness always."

" That's right !   Let us make the best of our mountain, for we are likely to enjoy its solitudes for some time to come."

" If only I could set my affections right ! " she said wistfully.   " Perhaps, as you think, I have better feelings underneath, but they are not on the top just now.   I am ashamed to be with Hermie, because I suspected her ; and father is ashamed. to be with me, because I am not good enough to forget what he has done.   And I have no comfort in religion, for either I think God is cruel, or else most likely it is all chance and there is no reason at the heart of the universe."

" You are quite ready to believe now in God's insanity."

" How can you taunt me in that way?   I have told you that I am ashamed of my wicked thoughts about Hermione. But how can we tell that there is any mind governing the universe ?"

" It was only when you could not understand your sister that you thought you had found any proof of lack of mind. You would treat the great Power that lies behind the universe in the same way."

" I have heard many good people say as much. Do you think it wicked ?"

" I can only say that I have never liked you so well since I knew your thoughts about your sister. How much more must all good spirits despise us when we distrust the mind of God."

" You speak unkindly. I cannot alter my doubt."

" No. You are endowed with beauty and health, intellect and heart. You have done many things well. But this, I suppose, is a radical defect."

She did not look satisfied. " How can I alter it ?"

" If I were you I would go on laying out the orchard you were working at in spring. You could put in a great many of the small trees yourself. I have gained so much from delving that I offer you the same occupation with a certificate of merit."

"But I can't get the rows straight alone," she said, "or prepare the ground. It is all as it was when the Godsons left. It was you who made me send them away."

"And now I have come to ask you to take young Godson back," he said. So he told the young man's story. "He will have time to help in the orchard if he is employed about your father."

"Do you think there is no risk?" she asked, with the grave dignity that the peculiar isolation of her life had given.

"I would not undertake to say that," he replied, with a smile. "But such as it is, he takes it. You need help sadly, and perhaps you will both learn more wisdom than I was able to impart when I first interfered."

Durgan went his solitary way down the trail. Godson was still waiting for him. He was as fine a fellow as those remote mountains produce —spare, tall, with a curious look of ideality peculiar to their hardy sons. When he was told he might go up to the summit house, his blue eyes, far under the projecting tow-coloured brows, looked almost like the eyes of a saint wrapped in adoration. Durgan was not in a mood to feel that Bertha was his superior.

Durgan built sticks for a fire on the rock-ledge to make his own coffee. He was a better man physically than he had been when he came to Deer Mountain—strong, sinewy, and calm, the processes of age arrested by the vital tide of work. Alone as he was in his eyrie, he could take keen pleasure in the stateliness of his rock palace, in the vision of nights and days that passed before it, in the food and rest that his body earned. To-night he was not expecting satisfaction, and when he struck his match the whole universe was grey and seemed empty; but no sooner had his small beacon blazed than an answering beam leaped out of the furtherest distance. It was the evening star.

PLYMOUTH
WILLIAM BRENDON AND SON
PRINTERS

LaVergne, TN USA
29 August 2010
195057LV00003B/56/A